The ES )f

STARTING YOUR OWN SMALL BUSINESS

LaRue Tone Hosmer
Wendell O. Metcalf
Lynne Waymon

Compiled and Edited by
Dr. M. Fogiel, Director

Research & Education Association
61 Ethel Road West
Piscataway, New Jersey 08854

THE ESSENTIALS ® OF
STARTING YOUR OWN SMALL BUSINESS

Printed in the United States of America

Library of Congress Catalog Card Number 98-65150

International Standard Book Number 0-87891-225-8

ESSENTIALS is a registered trademark of
Research & Education Association, Piscataway, New Jersey 08854

CONTENTS

Introduction:

"There's No Place Like Home"

The cottage industry, an old-fashioned enterprise, is enjoying a revival so strong that it's difficult to find out just how many Americans are now working at home. Estimates range in the millions.

Because women now enter business at a rate five times faster than men, the trend of operating from home is growing. A natural starting place for many businesses seems to be the garage, basement, or den. A recent Census Bureau study showed that numerous women's businesses are operated out of the home.

Homemakers, hobbyists, retirees, people interested in a second income, and the disabled are just a few of the groups attracted to home enterprises. A young mother's craft business began when she started appliqueing decorations on her children's clothes. A retired government worker bought 36 beehives and sold honey to local health food stores and at craft fairs. A teacher did typing and secretarial jobs for her husband and friends until she realized the potential market and opened a full-time secretarial service from her apartment. Others have become home business owners by using their skills in catering, counseling, teaching, day care, sewing, writing, photography, counsulting, market research, and landscape design.

The list of services that have been successfully operated from home is endless: chimney sweeping, maid services, messenger services, wake-up and answering services, home nursing, mail order businesses, party planning, dog grooming, kitchen and closet planning and organizing, and others too numerous to mention. As you explore the questions asked in the first chapter, "Home Entrepreneurship: Is It For You," let your thoughts run freely through the possibilities until you can target exactly the right type of business for your skills, your home space, your market, and your part of the country.

Home Entrepreneurship:

Is It For You?

The first step in deciding whether to start a business is to ask yourself this important question: "Do I have what it takes to be an entrepreneur?" Studying the characteristics of successful business owners will help you to tell whether your personality traits, experiences, and values are similar to those who have succeeded. And assessing your experience, skills, and life goals will also help you decide if you want to invest the energy, time, and resources that successful entrepreneurship requires.

Who is the "Typical" Entrepreneur?

What makes an entrepreneur successful is a hotly debated and vigorously researched subject. In *Success And Survival In The Family-Owned Business*, Pat B. Alcorn, an expert on entrepreneurial problems, has developed the following questionnaire to help you determine your "Entrepreneurial Quotient." Write your answers in the margin. Then read on to discover what she believes characterizes the typical entrepreneur:

Do you reconcile your bank account as soon as the monthly statement comes in?
_____
Entrepreneurs are careful about money. They usually know how much money they have so they can seize oppor-

tunitites on short notice. They know what things cost, whether prices are going up or down, and whether they are getting a bargain.

Did you earn money on your own from some source other than your family before you were 10 years old? ___
Most people who are going to make money in business show an affinity for making money at an early age—by babysitting, selling lemonade, delivering newspapers, or some such strategy.

Did you take part in competitive sports in school and do you continue to do so? ___
Entrepreneurs obviously have a competitive nature and many of them show this at an early age in sports activities. It is not so much that sports train people to be entrepreneurs; rather, the same inner drives push people to be athletes and entrepreneurs.

Do you get up early in the morning and find youself at work before others are out of bed? ___
Entrepreneurs sleep and eat enough to keep up their strength, but they don't usually tarry at these pursuits.

Do you tend to trust your hunches rather than wait until you have a lot of information on hand? ___
Hunches are judgments based on factors that cannot be quantified. A big part of entrepreneurship seems to be risk-taking based on these hunches.

Do you keep new ideas in your head instead of writing them down? ___
Entrepreneurs keep a lot of things in their heads, including their most creative ideas.

Do you remember people's names and faces well? _____
Ease in remembering names and faces is very important in the business world.

Were you good in "hard" subjects—mathematics, biology, engineering, accounting, and so forth—in school? _____
People who major in business administration in college are more likely to be successful entrepreneurs than anyone else. They prefer subjects in which the answers are conclusive rather than open-ended conclusions full of contingencies.

In school, did you pretty much stay away from such organizations as Scouts and student government? _____
Most entrepreneurs tend to be loners rather than joiners, unless joining is a useful tactic for making contacts and gathering business information.

In courting the opposite sex, did you tend to go for one person at a time as opposed to playing the field? _____
Most entrepreneurs preferred one person because to play the field would have taken too much time away from business activities.

Do you close deals with a handshake rather than insisting on written contracts and guarantees? _____
Good entrepreneurs are often comfortable with something less binding than written contracts. When the only bond is a word, it becomes a matter of honor, and no entrepreneur can afford to lose honor.

Do you devote considerably more time and thought to work than to other activities, such as hobbies? _____
Entrepreneurs may have some leisure time activities, but their principal hobby is their work.

A similar test was developed by John Komives, director of Milwaukee's Center for Venture Management. Again, write your answers in the margin, then read on to see the expert's answers.

Was your parent an entrepreneur? ____
Having a close relative who was an entrepreneur is the single most telling indicator of a successful entrepreneur.

Are you an immigrant? ____
There is a high correlation between immigrants and entrepreneurs. In this sense, "immigrant" includes not only those who were born outside the United States, but also those who moved from farm to city or from the Midwest to the West Coast.

Did you have a paper route? ____
The entrepreneurial streak shows up early in life.

Were you a good student? ____
Typical entrepreneurs were anything but model students and often were expelled from school.

Do you have a favorite spectator sport? ____
The best answer is "no." Entrepreneurs are poor spectators. They often excel at individual, fast-paced sports such as skiing or sailing.

What size company do you now work for? ____
The typical entrepreneur comes from a medium-sized company—30 to 500 employees.

Have you ever been fired?   _____

Entrepreneurs make poor employees. That's why they become entrepreneurs.

If you had a new business going, would you play your cards close to the vest, or would you be willing to discuss problems with your employees?   _____

Typical entrepreneurs have a secretive streak. If they confide in anyone, it is likely to be another entrepreneur.

Are you an inventor? A Ph.D.?   _____

Not a positive indicator. Inventors fall in love with their products, Ph.D.s with their research.

How old are you?   _____

The typical age for starting a business seems to be 32-35.

When do you plan to retire?   _____

Entrepreneurs don't retire. They may sell a business and think they will retire, but they are always out there starting a new business.

In still another study, Jeffry A. Timmons asserts that entrepreneurs are people who have high energy, feel self-confident, set long-term goals, and view money as a measure of accomplishment. They persist in problem solving, take moderate risks, learn from failures, seek and use feedback, take initiative, accept personal responsibility, and use all available resources. They compete with themselves and believe that success or failure lies within their personal control or influence. They can tolerate ambiguity.

Are You Ready, Willing, and Able?

Now that you have studied the characteristics of others who have succeeded, survey your reasons for wanting a home-based business. Are you dissatisfied with your current job? What are your skills? What is your business experience, especially in the business you want to start? What are your life goals? What resources do you have that might help?

Answering these questions will provide reality testing for ideas that can sound incredibly glamorous when chatting with friends or seductively attractive when you are irritated or bored by your present job.

Refer to the chapter, *"Checklist For Starting a Business,"* and answer the questions and discuss your reactions with friends and family. Or better yet, ask several people close to you to think carefully about you and fill out the checklist for you. Have you underestimated your abilities? Overestimated them? Sometimes an evaluation by a friend is more useful than a self-evaluation.

How does your family react to the idea of a home business? Will you expect them to help out? What changes would your business use of the house mean for them? Will you have to remodel to create a usable business space?

What resources are available to you? Will you start by keeping your job and "moonlighting" for a while? Do you have a small nest egg, inheritance, or retirement income to live on until you get the business going? Do you already own tools or machines that will help (for instance, a word processor for a secretarial business or professional cameras and a darkroom for a commercial photography business)? Are you able to go back to school for training if necessary? Have you built up a network of contacts and possible customers through your previous lines of work or will you be starting from scratch?

Answering these questions honestly and completely will help you assess not only your chances for success but also which type of home-based business to choose. For instance, if your past professional life and contacts are all in the educational, teaching, child-oriented school area, then you should have powerful reasons for leaving that and opening a mail-order seed business. Possibly a tutoring business or a tot exercise franchise would use more of your resources and networks. On the other hand, if your assessment of your life goals and preferences helps you realize that you are burned out from working with kids, then perhaps a business planning birthday parties could later be built into a general party planning and catering business. You would be using your old contacts to build a long-range business plan that focuses on a service business for adults.

The Advantages of Home-Based Business

Why have millions of Americans chosen to work and live in the same place? Why are cottage industries sprouting faster than we can count them? Some home-based businesses start by accident rather than by conscious design. Secretarial services, day-care centers, craft ventures, and the like may start out as weekend activities in the recreation room. After a while their owners are surprised to see how profitable or enjoyable the venture has become. The glimpse of a healthy market lures them into a full-time venture. This low-risk, low-overhead, gradual kind of start-up is very attractive to new business people.

Many home-based business people cite decreased commuting time and other lessened business expenses as advantages for working at home. If your place of work is just 30 minutes away, that's five hours a week in commuting time, many dollars in gasoline and car maintenance or transit fares, and untold stress fighting traffic. Getting out of the high-fashion rat race is a plus for many who dislike having to dress up and continually buy new clothes to feel comfortable in settings outside the home.

Homemakers—mostly women but also an increasing number of men—are choosing a home-based business in order to have a more flexible lifestyle and to be closer to family. A parent who has a home office can eat lunch with the children or more easily attend special school or sports events. The home-based business person has more control over work hours than someone with a 9 to 5 job. Night owls who like to work until 3 a.m. can then sleep late (remembering, of course, to turn on the answering machine and let customers know the business hours). On the other hand, early birds can work without the usual disturbance from the telephones.

The tax advantages of operating a business from home are numerous but sometimes complicated. Wise business owners keep careful records and work with accountants, attorneys, and financial planners to make sure they are filing for the legal maximum write-offs and benefits.

The Disadvantages of a Home-Based Business

If you were hard at work in an office downtown, it is unlikely that three children would come storming in to ask for snacks or that you would end up using the ironing board for a bookshelf or have to think twice about hiring others because they might resent working at your kitchen table. These are just a few of the problems that make the glamour of working at home fade fast. Some disadvantages of working at home can be minimized by self-discipline, by setting clear limits with family and friends, and by projecting a professional image. Other disadvantages "come with the turf" and just have to be lived with. If a delivery man comes to the door, you will probably be the one to interrupt your work and sign for the package.

It takes time and discipline to establish steady, at-home work patterns. Often it seems easier to water the plants or do the laundry than to call a client, design a new brochure, or prepare bills for customers whose work you've completed. Without the deadlines imposed by supervisors or peers, it can be hard to do the least appealing jobs on your list. To make matters worse, others may not take you seriously. Neighbors may stop by to chat or friends may call your business number knowing you will answer. Without supervisors or managers, you are the one who must set limits and plan your time. There also is the problem of isolation. While you are now your own boss, you won't have the chats, the parties, the companionship of fellow workers. Losing such social contact requires adjustments.

As the business grows and changes, the home entrepreneur has to put up with cramped or inappropriate space. No more simply putting in a request for a bigger file cabinet or a new copy machine; now you must visit showrooms or garage sales, evaluate features, compare prices, and probably pick the item up yourself.

Your teenager may resent having to keep the stereo low because you're meeting with a client in the next room. Your spouse may be irritated by having to fry that freshly caught trout on the backyard grill so your office won't smell of fish. Your son may not want to give up the recreation room pool table so you can cut out 100 doll patterns this weekend. Neighbors may comment on the extra traffic your customers create on their quiet street. Family privacy and lifestyle patterns may be disturbed. And you will probably find yourself wrestling with laws and regulations you never dreamed could exist before you went into business.

Your Professional Image

Developing a professional image may be hard if you work out of your home. Projecting a businesslike image is an important part of building credibility with your customers and contributes to your own professional self-image. Design a logo or have one designed; order business cards and stationery. Set regular business hours. Use an answering machine or answering service. If other members of the family also answer the phone, make sure they know what to say. Have a businesslike office or "showroom" if you meet customers face to face. Consider referring to your apartment number as your "suite number" or rent a post office box rather than using your street address. Such practices might improve your chances of doing business with potential customers.

Your Next Steps

Now that you have reflected on the characteristics of successful entrepreneurship and assessed your skills, experience, and life goals, it's time to plan your next steps. Ask yourself: Given the disadvantages of working out of my home, do I still want to? Now that I know more about what's involved in starting a business, is it still for me? Do I need further training or experience? Should I begin part-time in order to test the waters, check our market potential, or refine my product or service? Do I need more time to research possible products or services? Have I decided on a particular business? The next chapter will help you define your business, the market, and the price to charge for your product or service.

Others Have Succeeded—Why Not You?

A former teacher tells how she started her own tutoring business:

> I taught languages in high school for seven years. Whenever I needed a little extra money, or during summer vacations, I tutored individual students. As my reputation grew, people began to ask me if I could recommend tutors in other subjects.
>
> As my enthusiasm for teaching in public schools waned, I began to research the possibility of a tutoring business. I started one summer by turning my second bedroom into an office and having stationery printed. Summer is a peak time because parents hire tutors to help their kids catch up on subjects By the end of that summer I was managing 48 tutors in 23 different subjects or grade levels all over the metropolitan area. I hired a part-time assistant who worked at the kitchen table. We added other services, such as classes to help high-school students prepare for national exams. Operating from home was perfect for me since I needed to keep my overhead low and keep a good cash flow to be able to pay my tutors.

A computer programmer tells his story:

> I longed to get enough work doing computer programming so that I could avoid the long commute to work and be closer to my two young boys as they grew up. I started working in an office I built in the basement doing small jobs and working for friends in the business who were up against tight deadlines. When I got my first big contract, I took the leap and gave notice. Now, two years later I've established a good track record with clients and have hired two others who work at terminals in my recreation room. I like being able to work late at night after the family is asleep. And I enjoy being around when the kids get home from school. I don't need a fancy downtown office. If I meet with a client, I make sure it's at his office, not mine.

2

Answering The Big Question:

What? Who? Where? How? and How Much?

What's the perfect home business for you? You've listed your
skills. You've outlined your interests. You've described your
family's preferred lifestyle. You've come up with a business idea.
Next, consider such questions as: Are there customers for my
product or service? How do I know? How will I find them? Who
are my competitors? What will I charge? How will I promote my
product or service? Finding the answers to these questions is the
challenging and sometimes tedious homework that will help you
determine your chances for success, and whether you should look
for another more marketable idea.

What Is My Product?

"I bathe and groom poodles and small dogs." "I design, construct,
and sell roll-top desks." "I provide accounting services to small
business clients." "I make dried flower arrangements." "I teach
intermediate and advanced piano to children." "I design and implement direct mail advertising campaigns for small businesses
and nonprofit organizations."

The first step in creating a business is to decide what your product is. What are you selling? Practice writing a short, specific statement describing your product or service. Getting a clear idea of a business concept is one of the most difficult tasks in creating a business. Your statement may change several times as you experiment with the market and test your skills. Instead of "I make toys," you may want to narrow your product line to "I make wooden dolls." Instead of "I write software programs for small business needs," you may decide to tap into a big market and "provide training for employees of small businesses in the use of accounting packages." See how it feels to describe your product or service to family, friends, potential customers, and fellow business people. Is your description clear and brief? Can you say it with confidence and enthusiasm?

Who Will Buy It?

To develop and test your business idea, answer the question "Who will buy my product or service?" Make a list of potential customers: individuals, groups, segments of the population, or other businesses that need your product or service. If you are making fabric-covered lap boards for people confined to bed, how will you quickly and inexpensively find a market? Through hospitals or home nursing care organizations? Through craft stores by displaying them as gift items? In mail order catalogues? Is there a market avenue that will reach children? Ask friends and colleagues for help in brainstorming all the possible markets (customers) and uses for your product or service.

Who Is the Competition?

Your business planning must also include an up-to-date analysis of your competition. Why? Because you need to plan your market position—how you will fit into the marketplace. Will your product or service be cheaper or more expensive than that of the major competitiors? Will it be more durable? Will you be open during hours that your competitors are closed? What benefits can you build into your product or service that your competitors don't offer? Will you do rush jobs?

In planning your business, look for a unique niche that will give you freedom from strong competition or that will make your product or service more valuable than others in the market. If you plan to open a day-care center and find that none in your area is open before school, early opening might make your service more competitive. If you discover that local caterers have overlooked the office party market, you might highlight that in your brochure. The more you can learn about your competition, the better you'll be able to decide how to position yourself in the market.

Newspaper ads and trade magazines are other good sources of market information. Check also with the Chamber of Commerce, your county office of economic development, the Census Bureau, and business and professional organizations to gather market and pricing data.

Where Are the Buyers? How Can I Find Them?

As you become more familiar with the competition, you will also be discovering where and how to find buyers. Whatever the type of home business you want to open, you will need to do market research to determine if there are buyers for your idea, where they are, and how to find them. (And in the process, you will also be gathering information on pricing.)

Visit your local library to compile local and county statistics on the size and makeup of your market. (While you are at the library, check out some books on marketing research so you will know what you are getting into.) Also, check those of the following resources that might have data about your product or service or the people who would use it:

Encyclopedia of Associates. Gale Research Company, Book Tower, Detroit, MI 48226.

Ayer Directory of Publications. Lists trade publications by subject matter. Contact the sales, marketing, or research departments for buying patterns among their readers.

"Survey of Buying Power." *Sales, Marketing, Management Magazine*. July issue each year.

Thomas' Register. Lists companies by product and service line, organized geographically and alphabetically.

Directory of Business, Trade, and Public Policy Organizations. U.S. Small Business Administration, Office of Advocacy.

Department of Commerce Publications. Data User Series Division, Bureau of the Census, Washington, D.C. 20233.

County Business Patterns. U.S. Department of Commerce, Bureau of the Census. Available for each state.

When your marketing research is completed you will have 1) identified your potential customers; 2) found out all you can about their habits, needs, preferences, and buying cycles; and 3) decided how to reach them to generate sales.

How Much Shall I Charge?

Four main factors will help you decide what to charge for your product or service: 1) your direct and indirect costs; 2) the profit you want to make; 3) your market research data on competitors' prices; and 4) the urgency of the market demand. There is rarely an exact "right" price but rather an acceptable price range within which you will want to fall. Avoid the common mistakes made by many new business owners—charging too much or too little. Use several approaches to arrive at a cost and "test" the price. If your ego is too involved, your price may be too high. On the other hand, if you have the atitude that "this is just a little something I do in my spare time" or "anybody could do this," then your price may be too low.

Here is a formula for setting a fair price. Calculate your price using other approaches, too, before you make a final decision on price:

Typical Pricing Formula

1. **Direct Material Costs**—Figure the total cost of the raw materials you have to use to make up your item. Figure the cost of a group of items and then divide by the number of items to find the cost per item. If you can easily and immediately determine the material cost of a single item, fine. Some items are produced in batches, however, and it is easier to get an item cost by dividing the cost of a batch by the number of items eventually produced.

2. **Direct Labor Costs**—Figure what you pay to employees to produce the item (whether or not you have employees now). You must assign a wage figure, even if you are the only one producing the item. Take the weekly salary you pay someone to produce the necessary number of items and divide it by the number of items. Add this figure to the Direct Material Costs total.

$$\text{Materials} + \text{Labor} = \$\underline{\hspace{2cm}}.$$

3. **Overhead Expenses**—These expenses include rent, gas and electricity, business telephone calls, packing and shipping supplies, delivery and freight charges, cleaning, insurance, office supplies, postage, payroll taxes, repairs, and maintenance. The accuracy of your costing depends on estimating logical amounts for all categories of expenses. If you are working at home, figure a portion of your total rent or mortgage payment (in proportion to your work space and storage areas), or assign a reasonable, competitive rent figure for the same amount and type of space. List all overhead expense items and total them. Divide the total overhead figure by the number of items per month (or time period you used above). The answer is your overhead per item.

$$\text{Overhead} + \text{Materials} + \text{Labor} = \text{Total Cost/Item}$$

4. **Profit**—Include an amount added to the cost of each item so you won't end up just breaking even or making the employees' wages. Check your competition and see what they are charging. (Retailers generally double the wholesale price.) If your product is

a little better than the competition, charge a little more. If your product is comparable, price it similarly. Remember, you will get the profit from each sale, in addition to the salary figure. Add the profit figure you have chosen to the total cost per item to get your total price per item.

$$\text{Profit} + \text{Total Cost/Item} = \text{Total Price/Item}$$

Remember, the main purpose in operating a business is to make a profit. Don't undersell your product or service just because "I'd be baking cakes anyway" or "I'm just starting out" or "I work out of my home." If you have a new, rare, handmade product or personalized service, the demand may be so high that customers are willing to pay a little more.

Promotion

Promotion is an overall, long-range plan designed to inform potential customers about what you have to sell. Advertising is usually thought of as the paid communication part of the promotion program.

To develop a total promotional campaign you must answer these questions: 1) What image or message do I want to promote? 2) What are the best media and activities for reaching my potential customers? 3) How much time and money can I spend on the effort?

Develop a long-range, consistent program for building image and reaching customers. Your image should be reflected in your business card, logo, stationery, brochure, newsletter, telephone answering service, signs, paid ads, and promotional activities.

Word-of-mouth recommendations from satisfied customers are the very best promotion any business can have. Consider which promotional tactics will build the confidence and image you are looking for—giving speeches and interviews (often good for counselors, teachers, lawyers, consultants), having an open house or holiday home sale (for craftspeople), holiday recitals or shows (for music and dance teachers or day-care operators), free demonstrations and samples (for retailers, decorators, caterers).

Several small ads may have more impact than one large, splashy ad. Conduct a **campaign** rather than having a one-shot ad or event. If you hire a public relations firm, look for one that can give you personal attention and develop a total marketing plan for you, not just a couple of ads. The plan should include market research, a profile of your target audience, a clear description of the image they recommend you project, the written copy, and a list of media (including cost and scheduling calendars) that are best for your type of product or service. As a new small business owner, you will probably decide to set aside a certain dollar amount per year or a percentage of past, current, or projected sales for paid advertising.

3

Managing Your Business:

Structure, Recordkeeping, Taxes, and Insurance

You're The Boss.

A telling sign on a new businessowner's desk read: "Yesterday I didn't even know how to spell ENTREPRENEUR and now I are one!" Now that you have decided to open a home-based business, **all** decisions will be your responsibility, not just those you previously enjoyed because they involved your area of expertise. Of course, as a day-care operator you already knew how to soothe an upset child, but as the owner of that business, do you know when to file your taxes? As a consultant you have over 20 years' experience advising organizations on personnel matters, but do you know if it's to your advantage to incorporate? You are an expert at word processing, but do you know how to develop an efficient recordkeeping and billing system? You are the boss now and the good health of your business depends on your management skills.

Choosing Your Form of Business Organization

One of the most important decisions you will make is how to set up the business as a 1) sole proprietorship, 2) partnership, or 3) corporation. Remember, the small business owner **risks it all,** no matter what form of organization.

The forming of a business organization depends on the following factors:

- Legal restrictions

- Need for capital

- Liabilities assumed

- Number of people associated in the venture

- Kind of business or operation

- Tax advantages or disadvantages

- Intended division of earnings

- Perpetuation of the business

Most home-based businesses are sole proprietorships or partnerships, but a comparison of the advantages and disadvantages of each type of organization follows:

A sole proprietorship is the least costly way of starting a business. You can form a sole proprietorship by finding a location and opening the door for business. There are the usual fees for registering your business name and for legal work in changing zoning restrictions and obtaining necessary licenses. Attorney's fees for starting your business will be less than for the other forms because less document preparation is required.

Sole Proprietorship

Advantages	Disadvantages
• Easiest to get started	• Unlimited liability
• Greatest freedom of action	• Death or illness endanger business
• Maximum authority	• Growth limited to personal energies
• Income tax advantages in very small firms	• Personal affairs easily mixed with business
• Social Security advantage to owner	

A **partnership** can be formed by simply making an oral agreement between two or more persons, but such informality is not recommended. Legal fees for drawing up a partnership agreement are higher than those for a sole proprietorship, but may be lower than incorporating. You would be wise, however, to consult an attorney to have a partnership agreement drawn up to help resolve future disputes.

Partnership

Advantages	Disavantages
• Two heads better than one	• Death, withdrawal, or bankruptcy of one partner endangers business
• Additional sources of venture capital	
• Better credit rating than corporation of similar size	• Difficult to get rid of bad partner
	• Hazy line of authority

You can **incorporate** without an attorney, but you would be unwise to do so. You may think a small family corporation does not need an attorney, but an attorney can save members of a family corporation from hard feelings and family squabbles. Attorney's fees may run high if organization problems are complex. The corporate form is usually the most costly to organize.

Corporation

Advantages	*Disadvantages*
• Limited liability for stockholders (while true for big business, may not be for small business)	• Gives owner a false sense of security
• Continuity	• Heavier taxes
• Transfer of shares	• Power limited by Charter
• Easier to raise capital	• Less freedom of activity
• Possible to separate business functions into different corporations	• Legal formalities
	• Expensive to launch

Recordkeeping

Keeping accurate and up-to-date business records is, for many people, the most difficult and uninteresting aspect of operating a home-based business. If this area of business management is one that you anticipate will be hard for you, plan *now* how you will cope. Don't wait until tax time or until you are totally confused. Take a course at the local community college, ask a volunteer SCORE® (Service Corps of Retired Executives) representative from the Small Business Administration to help you in the beginning, or hire an accountant to advise you on setting up and maintaining a recordkeeping system.

Your records will be used to prepare tax returns, make business decisions, and apply for loans. Set aside a special time each day to update your records. It will pay off in the long run with more deductions and fewer headaches.

If your business is small or related to an activity that is usually considered a hobby, it's even more important that you keep good records. The IRS may decide that what you are doing is only a hobby, and you won't be allowed to deduct expenses or losses from your home-produced income at tax time. So keep records of all transactions in which you spend or bring in money. Pick a name for your business and register it with local or state regulatory authorities. Call your city hall or county courthouse to find out how.

Your records should tell you these three facts:

- How much cash you owe,

- How much cash you are due, and

- How much cash you have on hand.

You should keep five basic journals:

1. **Check register**—Shows each check disbursed, the date of disbursement, number of the check, to whom it was made out (payee), the amount of money disbursed, and for what purpose.

2. **Cash receipts**—Shows the amount of money received, from whom, and for what.

3. **Sales journal**—Shows the business transaction, date, for whom it was performed, the amount of the invoice, and the sales tax, if applicable. It may be divided to indicate labor and goods.

4. **Voucher register**—A record of bills, money owed, the date of the bill, to whom it is owed, the amount, and the service.

5. **General journal**—A means of adjusting some entries in the other four journals.

Choosing a Recordkeeping System

Set up your records to reflect the amount and type of activity in your particular business. There are a wide range of pre-packaged recordkeeping systems. The most useful system for a small, home-based business is usually based on what is called the "One-Write System." It captures information at the time the transaction takes place. These One-Write Systems are efficient because they eliminate the need for recopying the data and are compatible with electronic data processing if you should decide to computerize.

Even though you may be small and just beginning, it is probably wise to consult an accountant to help you decide which record-keeping system is best for your business. Once it is set up, you can record the daily transactions or periodically have a bookkeeper post your daily transactions in your General Ledger and prepare your financial statements.

Be sure to establish a **separate** bank account for your business— even before the first sale. Then you will have a complete and distinct record of your income and expenditures for tax purposes, and you won't have to remember which expenses were business and which were personal.

It is important to choose a recordkeeping system that you understand and will use. It will help you see how well the business is doing and is the first step in responsible financial management.

Tax Obligations and Benefits

Significant tax savings are available to the home-based business-owner in the form of deductions, credits, and depreciation allowances. The time, money, and energy you put into keeping good records and keeping current on tax laws will be worthwhile and ensure that you operate within the law. You will need to plan for income tax, social security (all self-employed persons must pay a federal self-employment tax), employees' taxes (if you hire anyone), property tax on your home and business-related taxes, such as sales tax, gross-receipts or inventory tax (in some states and localities), and excise or individual item taxes (on certain commodities).

The Internal Revenue Service supplies the following free booklets (and runs free workshops) to give you details on your specific obligations:

- *Your Federal Income Tax* (Publication 17)

- *Tax Guide for Small Business* (Publication 334)

- *Business Use of Your Home* (Publication 587)

- *Employer's Tax Guide* (Circular E)

- *Self-Employment Tax* (Publication 533)

- *Tax Information on Retirement Plans for the Self-Employed* (Publication 560)

- *Tax Information on Depreciation* (Publication 534)

- *Information on Excise Taxes* (Publication 510)

- *Tax Withholding and Estimated Tax* (Publication 505)

There are various federal and state forms you will need to fill out to start a small business. The federal government requires you to fill out several forms including the following:

- Application for Employer Identification Number (Form SS-4) (If you have employees or are subject to excise tax)

- Employer's Annual Unemployment Tax Return (Form 940)

- Employer's Quarterly Federal Tax Return (Form 941)

- Employee's Withholding Allowance Certificate (W-4)

- Employer's Wage and Tax Statement (W-2)

- Reconciliation/Transmittal of Income and Tax Statements (W-3)

As a home-based business owner you should be aware that every business decision—each purchase and transaction you make—has tax implications or built-in tax advantages or disadvantages. Deductions may be available for home maintenance and improvements; automobile expenses; telephone expenses; office and work space; inventory space; major purchases, such as a computer; and a wide variety of other items such as uniforms, coffee service, trademarks, a safe deposit box, credit bureau fees, and business cards.

Each business situation is different and tax laws change, so consult up-to-date references, a trusted attorney, and an accountant who can advise you on your particular obligations and benefits.

Insurance

Insurance helps to safeguard your business against losses from fire, illness, and injury. You cannot operate without it. Talk with an insurance representative about your business needs. Check with the insurance carriers on your home policy and make sure business use of your home is compatible with your homeowner's policy. In addition to a homeowner's policy (personal plan), now that you have a business, you will need a commercial policy for full protection. Discuss these other possible needs with your agent:

- Product Liability Coverage—to protect you in case your product causes injury to the user

- Auto Liability and "Non-owned" Auto Liability Insurance—if a car is ever used to support the business in any way

- Medical Payments Insurance—payable if someone is injured in your home whether or not it was your fault

- Worker's Compensation—if you have employees

- Business Interruption Insurance or Earnings Insurance—in case your business is damaged by fire or some other cause and you must totally or partially suspend operations

- Disability Income Protection—a form of health insurance in case you become disabled

- Business Life Insurance—to provide funds for transition if you die

Be sure to keep all your insurance records and policies in a safe place—either with your accountant or in a safe deposit box. If you keep them at home for convenience sake, then give your policy numbers and insurance company names to your accountant or lawyer or put it in your safe deposit box.

Final advice for the wise business person is to read **and understand** the fine print in all policies and to reevaluate business insurance needs about every six months.

Other Considerations

Another aspect of planning is sheltering tax dollars through a Keogh Plan or corporate pension and profit-sharing plans, if your business is incorporated, or a retirement plan.

If you have a partnership, consider making a Buy and Sell Agreement with your partner(s). This agreement requires the surviving partner(s) to buy, and the heirs to sell, the deceased partner's interest. The surviving partner(s) then becomes the sole owner(s) and the heirs receive cash for their share of the business.

4

Dealing With Laws:
Zoning, Licensing, Permits, and Others

Unfortunately, many home-based business people try to "slide" into business, saying "I'll just try it for a few months and see how things go" or "It's not really a **business**. I have only ten clients." This attitude can lead to a lack of planning and big disappointments. If you set up your studio, print business cards and flyers announcing classes, and then find that regulations make it illegal to operate out of your home, you may have to start all over.

Zoning

Before you start your home-based business, do a thorough investigation of the zoning laws in your community. Zoning regulations spell out activities permitted and prohibited in specific portions of a city or county. Call your town hall, zoning office, or local library to get a copy of zoning laws. Find out the structure of your local zoning groups. Most areas have Planning, Zoning, and Appeals Boards.

If the home business you are planning conforms to zoning regulations, then all you need to do is keep abreast of new proposals that may affect your situation. It's a good idea to stay in touch with others operating from their homes by joining business organizations or neighborhood groups in case you ever need to band together to propose or oppose new regulations. Maintaining a low profile and friendly relations with your neighbors will result in more support from them should adverse regulations affecting your business ever be proposed.

If through your research you discover that the home business you are planning would violate the zoning code, there are several possible ways to proceed. You might wish to check with an attorney who specializes in zoning law to look for a legal way around the regulation. You might decide to apply to the Zoning Board for a variance or exception. Or you may be able to change your business enough to make the operation fit the law. If the regulation outlaws businesses that employ people other than the owner at home, maybe you can have employees take work to their own homes. If your business will create too much traffic, consider another strategy for product distribution. If your business will create too much noise, maybe you can soundproof your house. At last resort, ask yourself "Is it worth it to organize a drive to change the law?" Considering the rapid growth in the number of home-based businesses, you just might find other entrepreneurs who are also interested in submitting a change in the regulations to the Zoning Board. Go to meetings of the Board and try to identify the person who appears most active and most sympathetic to your position.

In the unfortunate and unlikely (most zoning officers don't have time to chase people who aren't bothering anybody) event that you are issued a "cease and desist" order, you should: 1) file an appeal immediately with the Appeals Board (if you interpret the regulations differently than they do); or 2) submit a change in the regulation to the Zoning Board to allow your business, which may enable you to continue to operate without fines until the Board reaches a decision. You may need a lawyer if you are not entirely familiar with the regulations and the workings of the Board.

Cultural and national trends point in the direction of zoning regulations that allow quiet, nonpolluting, low-traffic kinds of home businesses. More and more corporations are employing people to work at home. Most neighborhoods will adopt a "live and let live" attitude if you keep your premises neat and quiet and don't create traffic and parking problems.

Keeping Up With Zoning Legislation

There are two ways to keep up with zoning legislation in your community (and with other topics of interest to home-based entrepreneurs). One way is to read local newspapers, especially the business section and the local or "neighborhood" sections. Be sure you notice local items about such things as proposed subway stations or the county's plan for revitalization. Changes like these could eventually influence zoning in your area. The other way to keep abreast of trends and zoning issues is to join the local chapter of a business group, such as the Rotary Club, the National Association of Women Business Owners, the National Family Business Council, or a Business and Professional Women's Club. Through newsletters, meetings, and friendships that develop, you will hear all the latest local (and national) issues discussed while you learn valuable business skills and make useful contacts.

Working With Professionals

Even the smallest and newest business needs help from at least two kinds of specialists: an attorney and an accountant. Depending on your type of business and your skills you may, from time to time, ask the advice of other professionals, such as a direct mail or marketing specialist, an insurance representative, management consultant, a computer specialist, a realtor, a public relations expert.

Several guidelines will hold true no matter what type of expert you are dealing with: 1) Interview professionals to see if you will be comfortable working with them. Make sure they have served other small businesses similar to yours. Find out ahead of time exactly what service you are buying, what the working relationship will be, and what fees will be charged. 2) Be completely honest about your business situation. Advice based on partial or incorrect information is no advice at all. If you are having problems, don't be embarrassed. If your sales are down, give the experts all the information you have and work as a team to solve the problem. If business is good, don't be afraid that professionals will steal your idea or expect a raise. Build a trusting, businesslike relationship. 3) Expect the professionals you hire to spend at least some of their time teaching you and explaining complex concepts. But don't expect to be spoon-fed or delegate all decisions to them. Take a course at the local community college in recordkeeping and taxes or public relations to develop more skill in areas where you are inexperienced. 4) Keep your appointments and pay your bills promptly.

Your Lawyer

To find a lawyer who is familiar with businesses of your size and type, ask for a referral from a business colleague, your accountant, the local Chamber of Commerce, your banker, or some other trusted source. Some local bar associations run a lawyer referral and information service. Some just give you names; others actually give information on experience and fees to help you match your needs to the lawyer's background and charges.

A lawyer can help you decide which is the most advantageous business structure (sole proprietorship, partnership, or corporation). He or she can help you with zoning, permit, or licensing problems; health inspection problems; unpaid bills; contracts and agreements; patents, trademarks, copyright protection; and some tax problems. Because there is always the possibility of a lawsuit, claim, or other legal action against your business, it is wise to have a lawyer who is already familiar with your business before a crisis arises. A lawyer experienced with your type of venture should also advise you on laws, programs, and agencies—(federal, state, and local)—that help small businesses through loans, grants, procurement set-asides, counseling, and other ways. He or she will tell you about unexpected legal opportunites and pitfalls that may affect your business.

In choosing a lawyer, experience and fee should be related. One lawyer may charge an hourly rate that, at first, looks cheaper than another lawyer's. However, because of a lack of experience in some area, the less expensive lawyer may charge a larger fee in the long run. Ask for a resume and check references. If you feel overwhelmed, take a trusted friend to the initial meeting to help you keep on track as you interview the lawyer about services and fees.

If you retain a law firm, be sure you understand who will work on your case and who will supervise the work. If junior lawyers handle your work, the fees should be lower. That's fine as long as you know an experienced attorney will be reviewing the case periodically.

Let your lawyer know that you expect to be informed of all developments and consulted before any decisions are made. You may also want to receive copies of all documents, letters, and memos written and received in your case or have a chance to read them in the lawyer's office.

Ask the attorney to estimate the timetable and costs of your work. You may wish to place a periodic ceiling on fees, after which he or she would call you before proceeding to do work that would add to your bill. Always have a **written** retainer agreement, describing just what you and the lawyer expect of each other.

Your Accountant

Most businesses fail not for lack of good ideas or good will, but rather for lack of financial expertise and planning. Look for an accountant as you would an attorney. Get referrals from trusted friends, business associations, or professional organizations. Discuss fees in advance and draw up a written agreement about how you will work together. Your accountant (along with your lawyer) can advise about initial business decisions, such as the form of the business. Your accountant will help set up your books, draw up and analyze profit and loss statements, advise on financial decisions (e.g., buying a computer), and give advice on cash requirements for your start-up phase. He or she can make budget forecasts, help prepare financial information for a loan application, and handle tax matters.

Accounting firms offer a variety of services. If this is not an easy area for you, the fees you pay will be well worth it. Most firms will maintain books of original entry, prepare bank reconciliation statements and post the general ledger, prepare balance sheets and income statements on a quarterly or semi-annual basis, and design and implement various accounting and recordkeeping systems.

They will also get your federal and state withholding numbers for you, give instructions on where and when to file tax returns, prepare tax returns, and do general tax planning for the small business person.

Your accountant is your key financial advisor. He or she should alert you to potential danger areas and advise you on how to handle growth spurts, how to best plan for slow business times, and how to financially nurture and protect your business future.

State and Federal Laws That May Apply to Your Business

Most localities have registration and licensing requirements that will apply to you. A license is a formal permission to practice a certain business activity, issued by a local, state, or federal government. You may have the type of business that requires a permit from the local authorities. There is often a small fee for licenses and permits (usually $15-25). A license may require some kind of examination to certify that the recipient is qualified. Your business name must be registered and a sales tax number must be obtained. Separate business telephones and bank accounts are usually required. Of course, you will want to have the latter anyway for accurate bookkeeping purposes. If you have employees, you are responsible for withholding income and Social Security taxes. You must also pay worker's compensation and unemployment insurance and comply with minimum wage and employee health laws.

If your operations are intrastate, you will be concerned primarily with state and local, rather than federal, licensing. Businesses frequently subject to state or local control are retail food establishments, drinking places, barber shops, beauty shops, plumbing firms, and taxi companies. They are primarily service businesses and are subject to regulations for the protection of public health and morals. Your attorney can help you make sure you have complied with all licensing and permit requirements. Depending on your type of business you may have to comply with building and safety codes, too.

Think twice about the liabilities of operating without proper licenses and registrations. If you begin to advertise or are fortunate enough to "make the news" in some way, you will probably hear from a local official. You will pay with embarrassment, time, and money if your business is not properly licensed.

If you find legal regulations, permits, and licenses confusing, make sure you find some way to get the information you need to operate legally. Get help from your lawyer, accountant, business partner, or even your local librarian. This is not an aspect of business operations that can be delayed until you "get around to it." Your business reputation and financial standing are at stake.

5

Understanding the Financial Side

Who Needs Financial Planning? You do! All businesses run on money for the purpose of making money. A major reason for business failure is the lack of financial planning. Although it is nearly impossible to make exact estimates, approximate ones will help. The very process of thinking through these financial questions will develop your business acumen and lead to solid planning. Get your accountant involved in reviewing your plans and advising you, too.

Estimating Start-Up Costs

Begin your financial planning by estimating your initial or start-up costs. Include all items of a nonrecurring nature such as fees, licenses, permits, franchise fees, insurance, telephone deposit, tools, equipment, office supplies, fixtures, installation of fixtures and equipment, remodeling and decorating, funds for your opening promotional event if you plan to have one, signs, and, of course, professional fees for your attorney and accountant.

Depending on your type of operation, the amount of money you invest, and the energy you expect to put in (part-time to full-time) can determine how much working capital you will need. Many business experts say if you expect a profit in six months, double that time and be ready to operate without profits for twelve months to give yourself a cushion in case of unanticipated expenses or delays. Study the growth patterns of other similar business and ask for advice from your accountant and attorney.

Projecting Operating Income and Expenses

Next, estimate the "working" capital you will need to keep operating for six to twelve months. Operating expenses include salaries; expenses for telephone, light, heat, office supplies, and other supplies or materials; debt interest; advertising fees; maintenance costs; taxes; legal and accounting fees; insurance fees; business membership fees; and special services expenses, such as secretarial, copying, and delivery service.

It is a good idea to obtain typical operating ratios for the kind of business in which you are interested. Among the sources for such ratios are Robert Morris Associates, Dun & Bradstreet, Inc., the Accounting Corporation of America, trade associations, publishers of trade magazines, specialized accounting firms, industrial companies (for example, National Cash Register Co.), and colleges and universities. The typical ratios for your type of business combined with your estimated sales volume will serve as benchmarks for estimating the various items of expense. However, do not rely exclusively on this method for estimating each expense item. Modify these estimates through investigation and quotations in the particular market area where you plan to operate.

In addition to business operating capital, you will need to plan for reserve capital to cover personal expenses. This estimate will include all your normal living expenses, such as food, household expenses, car payments, rent or mortgage, clothing, medical expenses, entertainment, and taxes for you and your family.

After you have estimated start-up costs, working or operating capital needed for six to twelve months, and personal expenses and obligations, you may see that you need more start-up capital than you thought. What will you do? Discuss this with your accountant, attorney, and trusted business associates and family. Entrepreneurs secure needed capital in a variety of ways. You can:

- Get loans or gifts from family members or friends. Make businesslike, written agreements and be sure to disclose fully the potential risk as well as the possible profit.

- Apply for a bank loan. For this you will need a comprehensive statement of your personal financial condition

and a business plan with financial projections to present
to the loan officer. If you need help in preparing your loan
application, take a course for small business people at a
local community college or visit your nearest SBA office
to get assistance form a SCORE® counselor. (SBA stands for
U.S. Small Business Administration.)

- Apply for an SBA loan guarantee. The SBA is not a bank,
  but it does extend guarantees and may rarely participate
  in a loan when the bank is unable or unwilling to provide
  the entire financing itself. The SBA loan officer will ask
  you the same hard questions as a loan officer in a commercial bank and require the same carefully considered
  data on your personal finances, start-up costs, and
  business projections.

- Search for some sort of venture capital. For start-up entrepreneurs some prior managerial or entrepreneurial
  track record is usually necessary in order to get venture
  capital. The main disadvantage of venture capital is that
  you will probably have to give up between 50 to 90 percent ownership of the new business in return for the
  capital. A home business is extremely unlikely to attract
  venture capital.

Understanding Your Balance Sheet

Your Balance Sheet is a summary of the status of your
business—i.e., its assets, liabilities, and net worth—at an instant in
time. By reviewing your Balance Sheet along with the Profit and
Loss Statement and Cash-Flow Statement, you will be able to make
informed financial and business planning decision.

The Balance Sheet is drawn up using the totals from the individual accounts kept in your General Ledger. It shows what you
have left when you pay all your creditors. Assets less liabilities
equal capital or net worth. The assets and liabilities sections must
balance—hence the name Balance Sheet. It can be produced
quarterly, semi-annually, or at the end of each calendar or fiscal
year.

While your accountant will be most helpful in drawing up your Balance Sheet, it is **you** who must understand it. **Current assets** are anything of value you own such as cash, inventory, or property that the business owner can convert into cash within a year; **fixed assets** are things such as land and equipment. **Liabilities** are debts the business must pay. They may be current (such as amounts owed to suppliers or your accountant) or they may be long-term (such as notes owed to the bank). **Capital** (also called equity or net worth) is the excess of your assets over your liabilities.

Prepare a Balance Sheet for your new business during the planning phase to estimate its financial condition at that time and also a projected one for the first year of business. This will help you decide on the feasibility of your venture and make modifications to ensure profitability. You can also use these statements as part of the documentation in a loan application.

Understanding Your Profit and Loss Statement

Your Profit and Loss Statement is a detailed, month-by-month tally of the income from sales and the expenses incurred to generate the sales. It is a good assessment tool because it shows the effect of your decision on profit. It is a good planning tool because you can "try out" decisions on paper before actually going ahead.

The Profit and Loss Statement includes four kinds of information:

- The **Sales** information lists the number of units sold and the total revenues generated by the sales.

- The **Direct Expenses** category includes the cost of labor, materials, and manufacturing overhead (but not normal overhead).

- **Indirect Expenses** are the costs you have even if the product is not produced or the service is not delivered. They include the fixed costs or normal overhead of salaries, rent, utilities, insurance, depreciation, office supplies, taxes, and professional fees for your lawyers and accountant.

- **Income** or **Profit** is the last category on the Profit and Loss Statement. It is shown both as pre-tax and after-tax or net income. The IRS will look at your pre-tax figure, whereas your loan officer and you are more concerned with your after-tax figure.

Your Profit and Loss Statement should be prepared at the very minimum once a year—and more often in the beginning or growth stages of your business. It is a key document from which the economic health of a business can be determined. Make certain you do it properly and understand its meaning.

Understanding Your Cash Flow Statement

Your business must have a healthy cash flow to survive. Cash flow is the amount of money available in your business at any given time. To keep tabs on cash flow, forecast the funds you expect to disburse and receive over a given period of time. Then you can predict deficiencies or surplus in cash and decide how to respond.

A cash flow projection serves one other very useful purpose in addition to planning. As the actual information becomes available to you, compare it to the monthly cash flow estimates you previously made to see how accurately you are estimating. As you do this, you will be giving your self on-the-spot business training in making more accurate estimates and plans for the coming months. As your ability to estimate improves, your financial control of the business will increase.

The creative business owner works with his or her accountant to use the information gleaned from all of these financial tools to make a variety of managerial decisions—decisions on buying supplies, expansion, when to hire more employees, how to get the best tax breaks, and many other important steps that will shape the future of the business.

6

Make It Easy On Yourself

Successful home-based business owners learn from experience—
their own and that of others. In Jeffry A. Timmon's study of entrepreneurial personality characteristics (*New Venture Creation: A
Guide to Small Business Development*), he notes that entrepreneurs
are disappointed but not discouraged by failure. They use failures
as learning experiences and try to understand their role in causing
the failure in order to avoid similar problems in the future. Furthermore, Timmons asserts, entrepreneurs seek and use feedback
on their performance in order to take corrective action and improve.

How to Learn From Experience

You can learn from experience in several ways:

First, work closely and creatively with professional advisors, such
as your lawyer and your accountant. As you continually review
your business records, you will see "mistakes," but you will also
begin to develop skill in planning and managing.

Second, continue to learn about all areas of business operations,
constantly acquiring new ideas. Most community colleges have
short, inexpensive, practical courses for business owners in topics
like "Financing a Small Business," "Choosing a Small Business
Computer," and "Starting and Operating a Home-Based Business."

Third, get to know other business owners with similar needs or
problems. Talking with others may be a way to avoid repeating the

mistakes they have made and benefiting from their experience. Local and national organizations offer membership, social events, networking opportunities, newsletters, and seminars for home-based business owners. Through these organizations you can often advertise your product or service to other business owners. They also provide a way to learn about services you may need, such as accounting, public relations, or a responsible secretarial service. These organizations offer updates in such areas as taxes and zoning in their newsletters and workshops.

Finding and Using Resources, Networks, and Support Groups

Start out with the attitude "Whatever my current business problem, I can find the solution. Somewhere there is information, a book, a person, an organization, or a government agency that can help." A word of warning though: finding resources and building networks can be very time-consuming. Joining organizations can turn out to be expensive, especially if you are too busy to use their services and support once you join. So use this list to organize your search for resources useful to you, then pick and choose carefully what you decide to read, join, buy, or attend:

Your Public Library: Visit your local library. Get to know its resources. In addition to books, many libraries offer free workshops, lend skill-building tapes, and become a central place to pick up catalogues and brochures describing continuing education opportunities for business owners. Ask the librarian for current copies of zoning regulations. Get familiar with new books and resources in your field (computers, health care, crafts, etc.) as well as in business skills (advertising techniques, financing, etc.) Look for magazines such as In Business, Black Enterprise, Venture, or The Journal of Small Business Management. Reading selectively is free. Subscribing to too many magazines may be expensive.

Organizations: A wide variety of local and national organizations have sprung up to serve the informational, lobbying, and networking needs of business entrepreneurs. Through meetings, services, or newsletters, groups such as the National Association of Women Business Owners, American Entrepreneurs Association, Business and Professional Women's Club, National Alliance of Homebased Businesswomen, and the National Association for Cottage Industry offer members everything from camaraderie to valuable "perks," such as group rates on health insurance. David Gumpert's book, *The Insider's Guide to Small Business Resources*, has addresses of many of these groups and other information on such resources.

Government Resources: Contact your local or district office of the U.S. Small Business Administration (SBA) to learn about SBA services and publications. The SBA also offers free or inexpensive workshops and counseling through SCORE.® SCORE® is a volunteer program sponsored by the SBA through which retired executives who have management expertise are linked with owners/managers of small business or prospective entrepreneurs who need help.

The Department of Commerce, Bureau of the Census, Department of Defense (procurement), Department of Labor, IRS (ask for the free "Business Tax Kit"), Federal Trade Commission, and the Government Printing Office all have publications and services to inform and support you. Local and state government offices may also have services to help you. Addresses will be available in your telephone book, under U.S. Government, at your public library, or at the SBA office near you.

Community colleges: Most community colleges now have short, inexpensive, noncredit programs for entrepreneurs. The classes usually are convenient to business owners and are taught by experienced owners and managers.

As a home-based business person you can overcome feelings of isolation and give and receive valuable information if you tap into networks and resources. Being active in professional and trade associations will help to build a good marketing network for your service or product. Take the time and invest the money for memberships. Then continually evaluate which organizations and resources best serve your business information and networking needs.

Managing Time and Stress

Expect to encounter stress and time problems similar to those of other business owners but accentuated by the fact that you work at home. Follow these guidelines to make it a little easier on yourself:

1) **Plan your time and establish priorities on a daily "to do" list**. Decide what your "prime time" is and do your most important or difficult tasks then. Set "business hours," specific times when you are at work and times when you turn on the answering machine because you are "on duty but off call." You, your customers, and your family will appreciate knowing your set routine, even though you know that for special events or emergencies you can break that schedule.

2) **Notice what your four or five big time-wasters are and learn techniques to eliminate them or compensate for them**. Some common ones are: telephone interruptions, visitors, socializing, excessive paperwork, lack of policies and procedures, procrastination, failure to delegate, unclear objectives, poor scheduling, lack of self-discipline, and lack of skill in a needed area.

3) **Stay in contact with people**. Even though you prefer to work at home, you should plan work-related or social activities that provide frequent contact with others. This will help your morale if you feel isolated. Even for home-based business owners who like feeling isolated, keeping up with business and professional contacts is a must.

4) **Build a fitness program into your day**. Many successful entrepreneurs exercise in order to think creatively because physical activity sends oxygen to the brain and helps the mind function better. With regular exercise your health will improve, your stress level will go down, and your trim look will inspire people to have confidence in your abilities.

5) **Give your home business as much of a separate and distinct physical identity as possible**. Although you might save a few dollars by using the ironing board as a bookshelf and a cardboard box as a file cabinet, the stress and strain of operating without

proper space and supplies will take its toll. Have a separate room or area for your business, with a separate entrance if customers or suppliers visit. Consider soundproofing so your family won't be bothered by your noise and vice versa. (In addition to the psychological and physical comfort of having a separate office, the IRS requires it in order for you to make a legitimate claim for tax deductions.)

6) **Take care of your major business asset: YOU.** Being the boss can be exciting, fulfilling, and rewarding. It can also be lonely, stressful, and demanding. Learn to balance your professional and personal life. Go on vacation. Get a weekly massage. Join a health club. Take a class in meditation. Attend a business owner's breakfast club. Your business depends on you to be at your best.

Profile: Jeanette's Day-Care Center

Jeanette wanted to return to work when her two children started school. Since her degree was in child psychology, she applied for a job as an assistant at a neighborhood day-care center. When she heard the salary, she decided there must be a better way. After several months of planning and researching, she decided to open her own day-care center in her basement recreation room. With remodeling she could accommodate the children and meet the zoning and licensing regulations. Four years later, her center has an excellent reputation and a long waiting list. She likes being "at home" and working in the business half-days while attending school for a graduate degree in business administration.

Profile: Wallflowers, A Wallpapering Partnership

Thirteen years ago Jane and Rachel bought a van together and formed "Wallflowers," a wallpapering and painting business. When they started, Rachel was recently divorced and wanted to test her entrepreneurial wings. She had quite a reputation with her friends for doing beautiful wallpapering and was often asked by them to help out on weekend remodeling jobs. Jane had little wallpapering experience but had handled all the accounting for her uncle's contracting firm and knew local suppliers and business owners.

They have never had to advertise. Word-of-mouth referrals have kept them busy ten months of the year. They close for two months in the summer so Jane can be with her kids and Rachel can go to Maine. Jane likes working "around" her family; if a child is sick or has a school program she'd like to attend, she doesn't have to apply for leave or fear losing her job. Her clients, mostly family-oriented people such as herself, understand that her children come first and the job will get done.

7

Buying A Going Business

To become the owner of a business you may decide to buy a going business. If you do, most of the same factors already discussed should be considered. But additional points must be checked.

Advantages and Disadvantages

Certain advantages may be gained in buying a going business.

1. You may be able to buy the business at a bargain price. For personal reasons, an owner may be sufficiently anxious to sell to give you a favorable buy.

2. Buying a business will save you time and effort in setting up your establishment with equipment and stock.

3. You may acquire customers who are accustomed to trading with the establishment. Thus you eliminate an initial waiting period for business while you are getting started.

4. The owner should be able to give you the benefit of his experience in the business and in the community.

Such benefits may be offset by disadvantages, however.

1. You may pay too much for the business because of your inaccurate appraisal or the former owner's misrepresentation.

2. The owner may have had a bad reputation. You would then be battling prejudices of former customers and, perhaps, of merchandise and equipment suppliers.

3. The location may be poor. (Before buying, the points concerning the selection of a location outlined in the preceding chapter should be checked. This is most important!)

4. The former owner's choice of fixtures and equipment may have been poor. Or they may be outmoded or in bad condition.

5. Too much of the merchandise or materials on hand may have been poorly selected.

How Much to Pay?

In deciding how much you should pay for a going business you should consider its profit potential. To be sure, the tangible assets, such as equipment and inventory, are important to you, but only to the extent that they contribute to future profits. If the seller is asking something for the intangible asset of good will take care in estimating how much it will add to your future profits. Furthermore, you must assess the cost of any liabilities you will be expected to assume.

Profit Potential

What you are concerned with is the *future* possibility of the business. Therefore, you should carefully estimate the sales and profits for the next few years. For how many years, depends on your expected return on investment. For example, if you expect a 10 percent return on your initial investment it will take 10 years to recover the investment. So, you would be interested in trying to forecast sales and profits for 10 years.

To estimate future profits you should start by analyzing balance sheets and profit and loss statements of the present owner for at least 5 years back. Going back 10 years would be even better. Some businesses may have inadequate records, but all should have copies of their income tax returns. What has been the rate of return on investment? Does it compare favorably with the rate you can obtain from other investment opportunities? How

does it compare with averages for other businesses of the same kind?

Have sales over the years been increasing or decreasing? What share of the market is the business obtaining within its market area? To find out this requires an analysis of the local market for the particular firm in which you are interested. What is the competition in the area, the population, the purchasing power? What are the trends? What is the outlook for increasing sales?

Are the profits satisfactory? If not, what are the chances of increasing them? Have profits been consistent over a period of years? If the last year's profit was unusually high in comparison with previous years, why was it? What is the profit trend? Have profits been increasing consistently or have they leveled off or started to decrease? What are the reasons for the profit trend, whatever it may be? Such questions should be answered to your satisfaction before you buy.

Study the expense ratios. How does the percentage for each expense classification compare with the average for the trade? The availability of average operating ratios for certain trades has already been mentioned. Comparison of the figures of the business offered for sale with standard ratios will bring out any discrepancies. In discussing these discrepancies with the seller you may become aware of operating problems which will help in making up your mind to buy or in deciding how much to pay for the business.

You will not necessarily be discouraged from buying the business if past profit records are not favorable. Very often the reason a business is for sale is because of recent records of poor earnings. Your examination may reveal that these have been brought about by poor management — and you may be convinced that your management will improve the situation. By the same token, an excellent past earnings' record, in itself, should not cause you to pay a large amount for the business without further investigation.

You should ask the seller to prepare a projected statement of profit and loss for at least the next 12 months. This means he will prepare his estimate of sales along with estimates of cost of goods sold and operating expenses. The seller has access to data about the business not available to you. However, this must be compared with your own estimate, recognizing that the seller's estimate of profits is likely to be less conservative than yours. With a detailed estimate of the next 12 months' operation you can compute working-capital requirements for each month. Then estimate the value of assets and liabilities as of the end of that period. Find the estimated return on investment. Do this by dividing the projected net profit by the price asked for the business. If you believe additional investment will be needed immediately to make the business run profitably, add this to the price. The highest price for the firm which brings you a return with which you are satisfied is the maximum price you will wish to pay. Thus an estimate of future profitability gives you the basis of a logical offer for the business.

If you are not familiar with accounting and income tax records, so that you may verify records of past operations and make a reasonable forecast of future operations, have an experienced accountant do this for you.

Tangible Assets

The most commonly purchased tangible assets are merchandise inventory, equipment and fixtures, and supplies. If the business you plan to purchase sells on credit you probably will take over accounts receivable.

What is the condition of the inventory you are buying? Is the stock of goods made up of timely, fresh, well-balanced selections of materials or merchandise? How much of it will have to be disposed of at a loss? A careful appraisal of the stock must be made. Each item should be separately priced and given a reasonable value. If at all possible, the inventory should be "aged"; that is, the length of time each group of items has been in stock should be determined. Then, the total dollar value of stock over 18 months old, 1 year to 18 months, 6 months to 1 year, and less than 6 months should be calculated. Usually, the older the inventory, the less value it has.

Equipment and fixtures should be carefully examined. Remember that you are buying second-hand furnishings with only a percentage of their original value. You must be sure equipment is in working order. Find out its age and obtain

BUYING A GOING BUSINESS
LOOK AT:

profitability

tangible assets

goodwill

liabilities

evaluations of similar equipment from dealers in new or second-hand equipment. Not only do you want to know how much equipment and fixtures have depreciated, but you must know how obsolete they may be. Office equipment may be in working order, but so obsolete that to use it instead of modern devices would be inefficient. Also, it may be difficult to obtain repair parts for old models in case of a breakdown. Many store fixtures quickly become out of date. New, modernized fixtures are necessary to attract customers. Machines used in factories may have been superseded by far more efficient equipment. To pay an exhorbitant price for the old type machine, no matter how good its condition, would be most unwise. You must make certain that all items of fixtures and equipment are fairly valued, after allowing for depreciation and obsolescence. Also, consider how much money is tied up in furniture, fixtures and equipment. Perhaps the business does not warrant the investment which the owner has made. And, finally, find out if there is a mortgage on any of the fixtures or equipment.

If you are taking over other assets, such as accounts receivable, credit records, sales records, mailing lists, or leases, investigate them closely. Accounts receivable should be aged to determine how many of them may be so old that collection will be difficult or improbable. Records and contracts involving favorable leases all have real value, and you should make certain that these are included in the sale.

Goodwill

Over and above the total appraisal of inventories, fixtures, equipment, and other assets, there will usually be an amount asked for good will. This is the amount which the owner is asking for the favorable public attitude toward his going concern. It is not to be confused with "net worth," which is the difference between the dollar values of the assets and liabilities of the business. Rather it is the ability of the business to realize a higher rate of return on the investment than ordinary in the particular type of business. When good will exists it is a valuable asset.

You should be realistic in determining how much you should pay for good will. No fixed formula can substitute for good judgment. Since it is payment for favorable public attitude, you should make some effort to check this attitude. You might question customers, bankers and others whom you feel have unbiased opinions. Then you must consider who will have the good will after the business changes hands. Does it belong to the business, or is it personally attached to and will it go with the seller?

A test of the payment asked is to compare it with past profits of the business. How many months or years will it take before the price of the "good will" can be paid out of profits? During that period you will, in effect, be working for the seller rather than for yourself. Another way of judging the value of this intangible asset is to estimate how much more income you will receive through buying the going business than by starting a new one.

Compare the price asked for good will with that asked for good will in similar businesses. In other words, if you are "shopping around" for a business, compare not only total prices asked, but the amounts asked over and above the reasonable value of net tangible assets. This will work in the reverse, too. If others are interested in buying the business, what they offer may determine what you will have to pay.

Liabilities

You should be sure that the seller pays off accumulated debts before paying the money agreed upon in the terms of the sale. Find out if there are mortgages, back taxes, liens upon the assets, or other creditors' claims. Obtain full information about any undelivered purchases. Although it is generally not desirable to assume any liabilities, it may be necessary in some instances. If liabilities are assumed, their value must be subtracted from the agreed-upon value of the assets to determine the net value.

The Price

After you have determined what you believe to be the net value this does not mean that you have reached the final price to be paid for the business. Value relates to what the business is worth. Other factors affect the final price. It is determined through negotiation and bargaining.

Endeavor to find out what the seller's reputation has been among employees and suppliers. Poor relationships may require extra effort on your part to establish a smoothly running organization. Make sure that suppliers will deal with you. If a franchise is involved, you should obtain satisfactory assurance from the supplier that it will not be withdrawn.

Why does the owner wish to sell? This should be one of your first questions. Is the reason given (such as a death in the family, poor health, or a needed change in climate) the really decisive factor? Or does the seller know that the neighborhood is changing so that need for his specific type of business will soon cease to exist; or that a new civic development, or zoning law, will affect the business unfavorably? You should search for his true reasons for selling by questioning not only him but others whom you know to be reliable.

Some business owners have sold out only to start a new business in competition with the buyer. Careful consideration should be given to placing limitations upon the seller's right to compete with you for a specific period of time and within a specified area.

Legal Advice

As a safeguard against costly errors, legal advice should be obtained before any agreement is made. The agreement should be drawn up by a lawyer to insure that it covers all essential points and is clearly understood by the parties. Among the items covered in a typical contract covering the sale of a small business are:

1. A description of what is being sold.
2. The purchase price.
3. The method of payment.
4. A statement of how adjustments are to be handled at the time of closing (for example, adjustments for inventory sold, rent, payroll and insurance premiums).
5. Buyer's assumption of contracts and liabilities.
6. Seller's warranties (for example, warranty protection for the buyer against false statements of the seller, inaccurate financial data, and undisclosed liabilities).
7. Seller's obligation and assumption of risk pending closing.
8. Covenant of seller not to compete.
9. Time, place and procedures of closing.

The seller and buyer must comply with the bulk sales law of the State in which the transaction takes place. The purpose of such a law is to make certain that the seller does not sell out, pocket the proceeds, and disappear, leaving his creditors unpaid. The seller must furnish a sworn list of his creditors and you, as the buyer, must give notice to the creditors of the pending sale. Otherwise the seller's creditors may be able to claim the personal property which you purchased.

As soon as possible after signing the contract, take possession. Otherwise, the seller may deplete the inventory and, in some cases, create ill-will for you.

8

Investing In a Franchise

MANY SMALL BUSINESS OWNERS have been helped in getting a sound start by investing in a franchise. You may want to consider such an investment. Franchising can minimize your risk. It will enable you to start your business under a name and trade-mark which have already gained public acceptance. You will have access to training and management assistance from experienced people in your line of business. Sometimes, you can obtain financial assistance which will make it possible to start your business with less cash than you would have needed otherwise.

On the other hand you must make some sacrifices when entering a franchised operation. You lose a certain amount of control of your business. You will no longer truly be your own boss in some situations. And, of course, you must pay a fee or share profits with the franchiser.

This chapter will present some of the advantages and disadvantages of franchising, where to look for a franchise and how to evaluate one. But, first, what is franchising?

Definition Of Franchising

Essentially, franchising is a plan of distribution under which an individually owned business is operated as though it were a part of a large chain. Services or products are standardized. Uniform trade marks, symbols, design and equipment are used. A supplier (the franchisor) gives the individual dealer (the franchisee) the right to sell, distribute, or market the franchisor's product or service by using the franchisor's name, reputation, and selling techniques. The franchise agreement (or contract) usually gives the franchisee the exclusive right to sell, or otherwise represent, the franchisor in a specified area. In return for this exclusive right the franchisee agrees to pay either a sum of money (a franchise fee), a percentage of gross sales, or to buy equipment or supplies from the franchisor — or some combination of these considerations.

Advantages Of Franchising

Some advantages of franchising to you, as a franchisee, are that you can start a business with:

1. *Limited experience.* You are taking advantage of the franchisor's experience which you might otherwise have to obtain the hard way — through trial and error.

2. *A relatively small amount of capital and a strengthened financial and credit standing.* Sometimes the franchisor gives financial assistance making it possible for you to start with less than the usual amount of cash. For example, the franchisor may accept a down payment with your note for the balance of the needed initial capital. Or, the franchisor may allow you to delay in making payments for royalties, purchases, or other fees in order to help you over the "rough spots." With the name of a well-known, successful franchisor behind you, your standing with financial institutions and credit associations will be strengthened.

3. *A well developed consumer image and goodwill with proven products and services.* The goods and services of the franchisor are proven and well-known. Therefore, your business has "instant" pulling power. To develop such pulling power on your own might take years of promotion and considerable investment.

4. *Competently designed facilities, layout, displays and fixtures.* The franchising company has designed effectively facilities, layout, displays and fixtures based upon experience with many dealers.

5. *Chain buying power.* You may receive savings through chain-style purchasing of products, equipment, supplies, advertising materials and other business needs.

6. *The opportunity for business training and continued assistance from experienced management in proven methods of doing business.* You can normally expect to be trained in the mechanics of the particular business, and guided in its day-to-day operation until you are proficient at the job. Moreover, management consulting service is provided by the franchisor on a continuing basis. This often includes help with record keeping as well as other accounting assistance.

7. *National or regional promotion and publicity.* The national or regional promotion of the franchisor will help your business. Also, you will receive help and guidance with local advertising. The franchisor's program of research and development will assist you in keeping up with competition and changing times.

All of these factors can help increase your income and lower your risk of failure.

Disadvantages of Franchising

Now, what are the disadvantages of franchising? Some of them are the:

1. *Submission to imposed standardized operations.* You cannot make all the rules. Contrary to the "be your own boss" lures in franchise advertisements, you may not truly be your own boss. In the first place, you must subjugate your personal identity to that of the name of the franchisor. If an important satisfaction to you is to have your business known by your name, a franchise operation is not for you. The franchiser exerts control and pressure on you (1) to conform to standardized procedure, (2) to handle specific products or services which may not be particularly profitable in your marketing area and (3) to follow other policies which may benefit others in the chain but not you. This means that you lose the freedom to make decisions — in other words to be your own boss.

2. *Sharing of profits with the franchisor.* The franchisor nearly always charges a royalty on a percentage of gross sales. This royalty fee must ultimately come out of the profits of the franchisee – or be paid whether the franchisee makes a profit or not. Sometimes such fees are exhorbitant – way out of proportion to the profit. The report of a Federal Government-sponsored study, entitled *The Economic Effects of Franchising,* showed that royalty payments ranged from a low of 1.0 percent to a high of 18 percent of gross sales in the fast food franchising industry. The median royalty fee was 4 percent of gross sales. The study revealed that a large number of fast food franchisors were misleading potential franchisees as to expected profits. Required purchases from the franchisor of merchandise, supplies or equipment might be obtained elsewhere for less. The study of fast food franchising showed that many franchisees who were required to buy a large proportion of supplies from their franchisors were paying higher prices than they could obtain on their own. Or, you might be paying more than other franchisees for the same services – a situation which exists in some franchising operations.

3. *Lack of freedom to meet local competition.* Under a franchise you may be restricted in establishing selling prices, in introducing additional products or services, or dropping unprofitable ones, regardless of local competition.

4. *Danger of contracts being slanted to the advantage of the franchisor.* Clauses in some contracts, imposed by the franchisor, provide for unreasonably high sales quotas, mandatory working hours, cancellation or termination of the franchise for minor infringements, and/or restrictions on the franchisee in transferring his franchise or recovering his investment. The territory assigned the franchisee may be overlapping with that of another franchisee or may be otherwise inequitable. In settling disputes of any kind the bargaining power of the franchisor is usually greater than that of the franchisee.

For example, the same study referred to above, showed that fast food franchisees worked a median of 60 hours a week, and some families as much as 120 hours. Alleged infringement of the franchisee's exclusive territory was a major source of friction between franchisee and franchisor. The power imbalance in favor of the franchisor is due not only to the franchisee's smaller financial resources but to his lack of information — information which the franchisor has. For example, the franchisor understands thoroughly the implications of the agreement he, himself, has devised and he has experience in negotiating under this agreement.

5. *Time consumed in preparing reports required by the franchisor.* Franchisors require specific reports. The time and effort in preparing these may be inordinately burdensome. On the other hand, you should recognize that if these reports are helpful to the franchisor they probably will help you to manage your business more effectively.

6. *Sharing the burden of the franchisor's faults.* While ordinarily the franchisor's chain will have developed good will among consumers there may be instances in which ill will has been developed. For example, if a customer has been served a stale roll, a burnt hamburger or received poor service in one outlet he is apt to become disgruntled with the whole chain. As one outlet in the chain, you will suffer regardless of the excellence of your particular unit. Furthermore, the franchisor may fail. You must bear the brunt of the chain's mistakes as well as share the glory of its good performance.

Minority Participation in Franchising

A number of franchise systems have developed special programs for minority individuals who seek to go into business for themselves. One such program asks the minority individual for only a 2 percent down payment. The franchisor matches this with 98 percent financing and up to a year of training. Another program is a joint venture between a minority-owned business and an established franchising company. The joint venture is not a merger of the two companies. Rather it is a plan whereby each company contributes an equal amount of dollars, but all responsibility for day-to-day operations is left with the minority-owned company.

In spite of the opportunities in franchise operation to help minorities, the Federal report on *The Economic Effects of Fran-*

chising, referred to above, foresees that "the relative level of minority participation in franchising at the end of the present decade will be little higher than it is at present."

Franchising can help the minority individual to start and manage a small business but it does not guarantee success. The challenges and problems of running a business remain whether or not the business is a franchising operation.

Finding Franchise Opportunities

Now that you've looked into what franchising is and considered its advantages and disadvantages where do you look for a franchise opportunity? Some of the sources are:

Newspapers. Classified sections of most daily metropolitan newspapers carry franchise offers under the "Business Opportunities" section. Sometimes the franchisor runs a "blind ad," not giving his name but listing a box number. This enables him to perform a preliminary screening in an effort to eliminate the "shoppers" from the "buyers."

Trade Publications. If you are interested in going into business in a particular trade seek out the trade publications for that trade. Franchisors advertise in the trade publications related to their franchised businesses.

Franchising Publications. Publications devoted strictly to franchising are another source of information.

Franchisor Exhibitions. Attendance at franchisor exhibitions, held in major cities, will give you the opportunity to meet franchisor representatives face-to-face and to compare a number of offers at one time. You should be wary of any franchisor who is willing to sign a contract on the spot. Your reason for attending is not to make commitments but to engage in give-and-take discussions directly with franchisor representatives and to obtain brochures and printed materials for further study.

Franchise Marketing Agencies. Franchise marketing agencies and franchise consultants serve to help prospective investors locate a profitable franchise. Also, they furnish information on the reputation and profitability of particular franchisors and their franchisees.

BEFORE INVESTING IN A FRANCHISE
CHECK:

The Franchisor

The product or service

The franchise contract

The market

The affect on YOU - the Franchisee

Franchising Companies. Once you have narrowed your interest down to one or two fields you can prepare a list of the top franchising companies in the fields and write directly to them for details. You should give some background information about yourself and the sincerity of your interest. Hastily and sketchily written inquiries are often ignored by franchisors.

Other Sources. While the above are the most important sources of information there are other direct and indirect leads concerning franchise opportunities. These include radio, television, direct mail, as well as suggestions from bankers, friends, business brokers, equipment and product suppliers.

Once you have located an opportunity in which you are interested, the next job is to evaluate it.

Evaluating A Franchise Opportunity

A franchise costs money. One can be purchased for as *little* as a few hundred dollars, or as *much* as a quarter of a million dollars or more. Hence it is vital that you investigate and evaluate carefully any franchise before you invest.

Beware of the "fast buck" artists. The popularity of franchising has attracted an unsavory group of operators who will take you if they can. Sometimes known as "front money men" they usually offer nothing more than the sale of equipment and a catchy business name. Once they sell you the equipment they do not care whether you succeed or fail. If you are promised tremendous profits in a short period of time, be wary.

The following check list will aid you in selecting the right franchise. Check each question when the answer is "yes." Most, if not all, questions should be checked before you sign a franchise contract.

Questions To Answer Affirmatively
Before Going Into Franchising

check if
answer
is "yes"

The Franchisor

1. Has the franchisor been in business long enough (5 years or more) to have established a good reputation? ____

2. Have you checked Better Business Bureaus, Chambers of Commerce, Dun and Bradstreet, or bankers to find out about the franchisor's business reputation and credit rating? ____

3. Did the above investigations reveal that the franchisor has a good reputation and credit rating? ____

4. Does the franchising firm appear to be financed adequately so that it can carry out its stated plan of financial assistance and expansion? ____

5. Have you found out how many franchisees are now operating? ____

6. Have you found out the "mortality" or failure rate among franchisees? ____

7. Is the failure rate small? ____

8. Have you checked with some franchisees and found that the franchisor has a reputation for honesty and fair dealing among those who currently hold franchises? ____

9. Has the franchisor shown you certified figures indicating exact net profits of one or more going operations which you have personally checked yourself? ____

10. Has the franchisor given you a specimen contract to study with the advice of your legal counsel? ____

11. Will the franchisor assist you with:
    a. A management training program? ____
    b. An employee training program? ____
    c. A public relations program? ____
    d. Obtaining capital? ____
    e. Good credit terms? ____

    f. Merchandising ideas? _____

    g. Designing store layout and displays? _____

    h. Inventory control methods? _____

    i. Analyzing financial statements? _____

12. Does the franchisor provide continuing assistance for franchisees through supervisors who visit regularly? _____

13. Does the franchising firm have an experienced management trained in depth? _____

14. Will the franchisor assist you in finding a good location for your business? _____

15. Has the franchising company investigated *you* carefully enough to assure itself that you can successfully operate one of its franchises at a profit both to it and to you? _____

16. Have you determined exactly what the franchisor can do for you that you cannot do for yourself? _____

The Product Or Service

17. Has the product or service been on the market long enough to gain good consumer acceptance? _____

18. Is it priced competitively? _____

19. Is it the type of item or service which the same consumer customarily buys more than once? _____

20. Is it an all-year seller in contrast to a seasonal one? _____

21. Is it a staple item in contrast to a fad? _____

22. Does it sell well elsewhere? _____

23. Would you buy it on its merits? _____

24. Will it be in greater demand five years from now? _____

25. If it is a product rather than a service:

    a. Is it packaged attractively? _____

    b. Does it stand up well in use? _____

    c. Is it easy and safe to use? _____

    d. Is it patented? _____

e. Does it comply with all applicable laws? ____

f. Is it manufactured under certain quality standards? ____

g. Do these standards compare favorably with similar products on the market? ____

h. If the product must be purchased exclusively from the franchisor or a designated supplier, are the prices to you, as the franchisee, competitive? ____

The Franchise Contract

26. Does the franchise fee seem reasonable? ____

27. Do continuing royalties or percent of gross sales payment appear reasonable? ____

28. Is the total cash investment required and the terms for financing the balance satisfactory? ____

29. Does the cash investment include payment for fixtures and equipment? ____

30. If you will be required to participate in company sponsored promotion and publicity by contributing to an "advertising fund," will you have the right to veto any increase in contributions to the "fund?" ____

31. If the parent company's product or service is protected by patent or liability insurance, is the same protection extended to you? ____

32. Are you free to buy the amount of merchandise you believe you need rather than being required to purchase a certain amount? ____

33. Can you, as the franchisee, return merchandise for credit? ____

34. Can you engage in other business activities? ____

35. If there is an annual sales quota, can you retain your franchise if it is not met?   _____

36. Does the contract give you an exclusive territory for the length of the franchise?   _____

37. Is your territory protected?   _____

38. Is the franchise agreement renewable?   _____

39. Can you terminate your agreement if you are not happy for some reason?   _____

40. Is the franchisor prohibited from selling the franchise out from under you?   _____

41. May you sell the business to whomever you please?   _____

42. If you sell your franchise, will you be compensated for the goodwill you have built into the business?   _____

43. Does the contract obligate the franchisor to give you continuing assistance after you are operating the business?   _____

44. Are you permitted a choice in determining whether you will sell any new product or service introduced by the franchisor after you have opened your business?   _____

45. Is there anything with respect to the franchise or its operation which would make you ineligible for special financial assistance or other benefits accorded to small business concerns by Federal, State, or local governments?   _____

46. Did your lawyer approve the franchise contract after he studied it paragraph by paragraph?   _____

47. Is the contract free and clear of requirements which would call upon you to take any steps which are, according to your lawyer, unwise or illegal in your state, county or city?   _____

48. Does the contract cover all aspects of your agreement with the franchisor? ___

49. Does it really benefit both you and the franchisor? ___

Your Market

50. Are the territorial boundaries of your market completely, accurately and understandably defined? ___

51. Have you made any study to determine whether the product or service you propose to sell has a market in your territory at the prices you will have to charge? ___

52. Does the territory provide an adequate sales potential? ___

53. Will the population in the territory given you increase over the next 5 years? ___

54. Will the average per capita income in the territory remain the same or increase over the next 5 years? ___

55. Is existing competition in your territory for the product or service not too well entrenched? ___

YOU — The Franchisee

56. Do you know where you are going to get the equity capital you will need? ___

57. Have you compared what it would take to start your own similar business with the price you must pay for the franchise? ___

58. Have you made a business plan — for example:

    a. Have you worked out what income from sales or services you can reasonably expect in the first 6 months? The first year? The second year? ___

    b. Have you made a forecast of expenses including a regular salary for yourself? ___

59. Are you prepared to give up some independence of action to secure the advantages offered by the franchise? _____
60. Are you capable of accepting supervision, even though you will presumably be your own boss? _____
61. Are you prepared to accept rules and regulations with which you may not agree? _____
62. Can you afford the period of training involved? _____
63. Are you ready to spend much or all of the remainder of your business life with this franchisor, offering his product or service to the public? _____

Conclusion

In conclusion, franchising creates distinct opportunities for the prospective small business owner. Without franchising it is doubtful that thousands of small business investors could ever have started. The American consumer might well have been denied ready access to many products and services. The system permits these goods and services to be marketed without the vast sums of money and number of managerial people possessed only by large corporations. Therefore, it opens up economic opportunities for the small business.

But not even the help of a good franchisor can guarantee success. You will still be primarily responsible for the success or failure of your venture. As in any other type of business your return will be related directly to the amount and effectiveness of your investment in time and money.

Because of this, most of the suggestions and information in other chapters of this book are appropriate even though you plan to operate under a franchise.

9

Setting Goals And Keeping Up To Date

Y OU NOW HAVE a broad, but sketchy idea of what is involved in starting your own business. There are definite disadvantages, as well as advantages, to such a venture. It is filled with risks. But knowledge and sound planning can minimize these risks. Diligent effort in searching out answers to questions such as those posed in this booklet is necessary to obtain the knowledge and make a sound business plan. This booklet has given you a start, and some suggestions toward answering the following questions:

Are you the type?
What business should you choose?
What are your chances for success?
What will be your return on investment?
How much money will you need?
Where can you get the money?
Should you share ownership with others?
Where should you locate?
Should you buy a going business?

How much should you pay for it?

Should you invest in a franchise?

Have you worked out plans for buying?

How will you price your products and services?

What selling methods will you use?

How will you select and train personnel?

What other management problems will you face?

What records will you keep?

What laws will affect you?

How will you handle taxes and insurance?

And now, in conclusion, two more are added. These are:

Will you set measurable goals for yourself?

Will you keep up to date?

Setting Goals

Setting the right kind of goals is a method for increasing achievement motivation. Such motivation must be sustained if you are to be successful in starting and running your own business. Set goals for yourself for the accomplishment of the many tasks necessary in starting and managing your business. Be specific. Write down the goals in terms of performances which can be measured. Major goals should be broken down into sub-goals, showing what you expect to achieve in the next 2 to 3 months, the next 6 months, the next year, and the next 5 years. Beside each goal and sub-goal place a specific date showing when it is to be achieved.

Plan the action you must take to attain the goals. While the effort required to reach each sub-goal should be great enough to challenge you, it should not be so great or unreasonable to discourage you. Take care not to plan too much action to reach too many goals all at one time. You must establish priorities.

Be sure you plan how to measure results so that you can know exactly how well you are doing. This is what is meant by "measurable" goals. If you can't keep score as you go along you are likely to lose motivation. Re-work your plan of action to allow for obstacles which may stand in your way. Try to foresee obstacles and plan ways to avert or minimize them.

GOALS IN YOUR BUSINESS PLAN

Generate measurable goals
and sub-goals

Organize action steps to
achieve goals

Allow for obstacles

Line up actual performance
against goals

Set new goals and sub-goals
to keep up to date

To help prospective owner-managers of small firms SBA has developed publications on the business plan. These publications are narrative and worksheets and are designed to be used in gathering and evaluating facts and figures.

Setting goals should include developing a specific plan for the business you hope to start and manage. Such planning helps you to avoid mistakes before you invest money in the business.

Even though you are careful in establishing realistic goals, unanticipated events may occur or new opportunities may develop. You may find it expedient to modify your goals and re-set your sub-goals. You must, then, do what is needed to bring your business plan up to date.

Keeping Up To Date

To keep up to date continue to look for information before and after you start your business. Get all the pertinent facts from everybody you can. Some of your sources are:

Your own customers.
Merchandise and equipment suppliers with whom you deal.
Trade associations and trade papers.
Commercial and industrial banks.
Chambers of commerce.
Better business bureaus.
Credit bureaus.
Business sections of libraries.
Minority economic and business development centers.
The United States Small Business Administration.

Visit your nearest United States Small Business Administration field office to consult with the business specialists. You will learn of other publications and sources of information which cannot be covered in this short book.

As a final step, before embarking upon your enterprise, review the checklist in the next chapter. You will find you have much work ahead of you in starting and managing your own business. But if you are the right person, you can succeed. Our American

KEEPING UP TO DATE

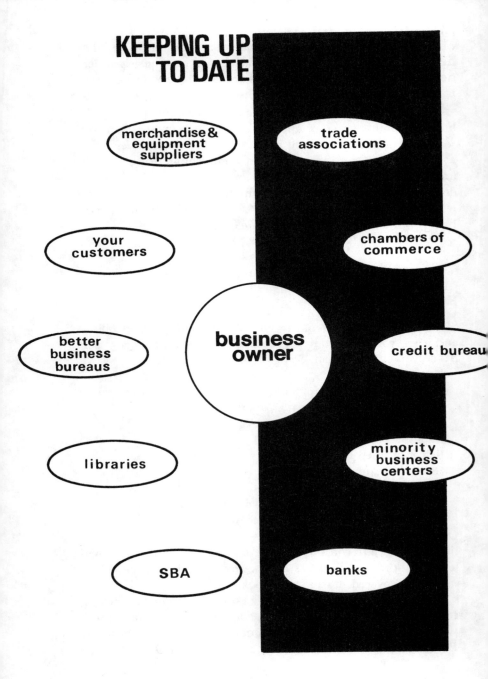

merchandise & equipment suppliers

trade associations

your customers

chambers of commerce

better business bureaus

business owner

credit bureau

libraries

minority business centers

SBA

banks

free enterprise system has flourished because of the opportunities it offers to be boss, run the business, make the decisions, and keep the profits.

10

Checklist For Starting A Business

Checklist
For Starting A Business

B EFORE ACTUALLY STARTING a business answer the following questions. The more of them you check as "yes," the better off you will be. All of them may not apply to your particular situation but, in all probability, most of them will. By the same token, the list does not cover everything. No list could for all types of situations in all kinds of businesses. You may wish to add some questions. Careful thought in advance will help to prevent mistakes and to avoid the loss of your savings. So many things must be considered that, unless some check list is followed, there is danger of significant matters being overlooked. And once you have started your business the urgency of day-to-day details reduces the opportunity for thoughtful consideration of all important questions.

Consider each question as it applies to your particular situation. Only after you have made an honest effort to answer a question favorably should you place a check mark in the right-hand column. Before deciding to ignore a question, completely satisfy yourself that it does not apply to your operation or that the action required is definitely not necessary.

Are You The Type?

Have you rated your personal qualifications using a scale similar to that presented in this book?   _____

Have you had some objective evaluators rate you on such scales?   _____

Have you carefully considered your weak points and taken steps to improve them or to find an associate whose strong points will compensate for them?   _____

What Business Should You Choose?

Have you written a summary of your background and experience to help you in making this decision?   _____

Have you considered your hobbies and what you would like to do?   _____

Does anyone want the services you can perform?   _____

Have you studied surveys and/or sought advice and counsel to find out what fields of business may be expected to expand?   _____

Have you considered working for someone else to gain more experience?   _____

What Are Your Chances For Success?

Are general business conditions good?   _____

Are business conditions good in the city and neighborhood where you plan to locate?   _____

Are current conditions good in the line of business you plan to start?   _____

What Will Be Your Return On Investment?

Do you know the typical return on investment in the line of business you plan to start?   _____

Have you determined how much you will have to invest in your business?   _____

Are you satisfied that the rate of return on the money you invest in the business will be greater than the rate you would probably receive if you invested the money elsewhere? ____

How Much Money Will You Need?

Have you filled out worksheets similar to those shown in this book? ____

In filling out the worksheets have you taken care not to over-estimate income? ____

Have you obtained quoted prices for equipment and supplies you will need? ____

Do you know the costs of goods which must be in your inventory? ____

Have you estimated expenses only after checking rents, wage scales, utility and other pertinent costs in the area where you plan to locate? ____

Have you found what percentage of your estimated sales your projected inventory and each expense item is and compared each percentage with the typical percentage for your line of business? ____

Have you added an additional amount of money to your estimates to allow for unexpected contingencies? ____

Where Can You Get The Money?

Have you counted up how much money of your own you can put into the business? ____

Do you know how much credit you can get from your suppliers — the people you will buy from? ____

Do you know where you can borrow the rest of the money you need to start your business? ____

Have you selected a progressive bank with the credit services you may need? ____

Have you talked to a banker about your plans? ____

Does the banker have an interested, helpful attitude toward your problems? ____

Should You Share Ownership With Others?

If you need a partner with money or know-how that you don't have, do you know someone who will fit — someone you can get along with?

Do you know the good and bad points about going it alone, having a partner, and incorporating your business

Have you talked to a lawyer about it?

Where Should You Locate?

Have you studied the make-up of the population in the city or town where you plan to locate?

Do you know what kind of people will want to buy what you plan to sell?

Do people like that live in the area where you want to locate?

Have you checked the number, type and size of competitors in the area?

Does the area need another business like the one you plan to open?

Are employees available?

Have you checked and found adequate: utilities, parking facilities, police and fire protection, available housing, schools and other cultural and community activities?

Do you consider costs of the location reasonable in terms of taxes and average rents?

Is there sufficient opportunity for growth and expansion?

Have you checked the relative merits of the various shopping areas within the city, including shopping centers?

8 9780878912254

check if answer is "yes"

In selecting the actual site have you compared it with others? ____
Have you had a lawyer check the lease and zoning? ____

Should You Buy a Going Business?

Have you considered the advantages and disadvantages of buying a going business? ____

Have you compared what it would cost to equip and stock a new business with the price asked for the business you are considering buying? ____

How Much Should You Pay For It?

Have you estimated future sales and profits of the going business for the next few years? ____

Are your estimated future profits satisfactory? ____

Have you looked at past financial statements of the business to find the return on investment, sales and profit trends? ____

Have you verified the owner's claims about the business with reports from an independent accountant's analysis of the figures? ____

Is the inventory you will purchase a good buy? ____

Are equipment and fixtures fairly valued? ____

If you plan to buy the accounts receivable are they worth the asking price? ____

Have you been careful in your appraisal of the companies good will? ____

Are you prepared to assume the company's liabilities and are the creditors agreeable? ____

Have you learned why the present owner wants to sell? ____

Have you found out about the present owner's reputation with his employees and suppliers? ____

Have you consulted a lawyer to be sure that the title is good? _____

Has your lawyer checked to find out if there is any lien against the assets you are buying? _____

Has your lawyer drawn up an agreement covering all essential points including a seller's warranty for your protection against false statements? _____

Should You Invest in a Franchise?

Have you considered how the advantages and disadvantages of franchising apply to you? _____

Have you made a thorough search to find the right franchise opportunity? _____

Have you evaluated the franchise by answering the questions in chapter 8? _____

Have You Worked Out Plans for Buying?

Have you estimated what share of the market you think you can get? _____

Do you know how much or how many of each item of merchandise you will buy to open your business? _____

Have you found suppliers who will sell you what you need at a good price? _____

Do you have a plan for finding out what your customers want? _____

Have you set up a model stock assortment to follow in your buying? _____

Have you worked out stock control plans to avoid over-stocks, under-stocks, and out-of-stocks? _____

Do you plan to buy most of your stock from a few suppliers rather than a little from many, so that those you buy from will want to help you succeed? _____

How Will You Price Your Products and Services?

Have you decided upon your price ranges? _____

Do you know how to figure what you should charge to cover your costs? _____

Do you know what your competitors charge? _____

What Selling Methods Will You Use?

Have you studied the selling and sales promotion methods of competitors? _____

Have you studied why customers buy your type of product or service? _____

Have you thought about why you like to buy from some salesmen while others turn you off? _____

Have you decided what your methods of selling will be? _____

Have you outlined your sales promotion policy? _____

How Will You Select and Train Personnel?

If you need to hire someone to help you, do you know where to look? _____

Do you know what kind of person you need? _____

Have you written a job description for each person you will need? _____

Do you know the prevailing wage scales? _____

Do you have a plan for training new employees? _____

Will you continue training through good supervision? _____

What Other Management Problems Will You Face?

Do you plan to sell for credit? _____

If you do, do you have the extra capital necessary to carry accounts receivable? _____

Have you made a policy for returned goods? _____

Have you planned how you will make deliveries? _____

Have you considered other policies which must be made in your particular business? _____

Have you made a plan to guide yourself in making the best use of your time and effort? _____

What Records Will You Keep?

Have you planned a system of records that will keep track of your income and expenses, what you owe other people, and what other people owe you? _____

Have you worked out a way to keep track of your inventory so that you will always have enough on hand for your customers but not more than you can sell? _____

Have you planned on how to keep your payroll records and take care of tax reports and payments? _____

Do you know what financial statements you should prepare? _____

Do you know how to use these financial statements? _____

Have you obtained standard operating ratios for your type of business which you plan to use as guides? _____

Do you know an accountant who will help you with your records and financial statements? _____

What Laws Will Affect You?

Have you checked with the proper authorities to find out what, if any, licenses to do business are necessary? _____

Do you know what police and health regulations apply to your business? _____

Will your operations be subject to interstate commerce regulations? If so, do you know to which ones? _____

Have you received advice from your lawyer regarding your responsibilities under Federal and state laws and local ordinances? _____

How Will You Handle Taxes and Insurance?

Have you worked out a system for handling the withholding tax for your employees?

____

Have you worked out a system for handling sales taxes? Excise taxes?

____

Have you planned an adequate record system for the efficient preparation of income tax forms?

____

Have you prepared a worksheet for meeting tax obligations?

____

Have you talked with an insurance agent about what kinds of insurance you will need and how much it will cost?

____

Will You Set Measurable Goals for Yourself?

Have you set goals and sub-goals for yourself?

____

Have you specified dates when each goal is to be achieved?

____

Are these realistic goals; that is, will they challenge you but at the same time not call for unreasonable accomplishment?

____

Are the goals specific so that you can measure performance?

____

Have you developed a business plan, using one of the SBA *Aids* to record your ideas, facts, and figures?

____

Have you allowed for obstacles?

____

Will You Keep Up to Date?

Have you made plans to keep up with improvements in your trade or industry?

____

Have you prepared a business plan which will be amended as circumstances demand?

____

11

Venture Capital for Small Business

Summary

Small businesses never seem to have enough money.
Bankers and suppliers, naturally, are important in
financing small business growth through loans and
credit, but an equally important source of long term
growth capital is the venture capital firm. Venture
capital financing may have an extra bonus, for if a
small firm has an adequate equity base, banks are
more willing to extend credit.

This *Aid* discusses what venture capital firms look for
when they analyze a company and its proposal for investment, the kinds of conditions venture firms may
require in financing agreements, and the various types
of venture capital investors. It stresses the importance
of formal financial planning as the first step to getting
venture capital financing.

What Venture Capital Firms Look For

One way of explaining the different ways in which banks and venture capital firms evaluate a small business seeking funds, put simply, is: Banks look at its immediate future, but are most heavily influenced by its past. Venture capitalists look to its longer run future.

To be sure, venture capital firms and individuals are interested in many of the same factors that influence bankers in their analysis of loan applications from smaller companies. All financial people want to know the results and ratios of past operations, the amount and intended use of the needed funds, and the earnings and financial condition of future projections. But venture capitalists look much more closely at the features of the product and the size of the market than do commercial banks.

Banks are creditors. They're interested in the product/market position of the company to the extent they look for assurance that this service or product can provide steady sales and generate sufficient cash flow to repay the loan. They look at projections to be certain that owner/managers have done their homework.

Venture capital firms are owners. They hold stock in the company, adding their invested capital to its equity base. Therefore, they examine existing or planned products or services and the potential markets for them with extreme care. They invest only in firms they believe can rapidly increase sales and generate substantial profits.

Why? Because venture capital firms invest for long-term capital, not for interest income. A common estimate is that they look for **three to five times their investment** in five or seven years.

Of course venture capitalists don't realize capital gains on all their investments. Certainly they don't make capital gains of 300% to 500% except on a very limited portion of their total investments. But their intent is to find venture projects with this appreciation potential to make up for investments that aren't successful.

Venture capital is a risky business, because it's difficult to judge the worth of early stage companies. So most venture capital firms set rigorous policies for venture proposal size, maturity of the seeking company, requirements and evaluation procedures to reduce risks, since their investments are unprotected in the event of failure.

Size of the Venture Proposal. Most venture capital firms are interested in investment projects requiring an investment of $250,000 to $1,500,000. Projects requiring under $250,000 are of limited interest because of the high cost of investigation and administration; however, some venture firms will consider smaller proposals, if the investment is intriguing enough.

The typical venture capital firm receives over 1,000 proposals a year. Probably 90% of these will be rejected quickly because they don't fit the established geographical, technical, or market area policies of the firm—or **because they have been poorly prepared.**

The remaining 10% are investigated with care. These investigations are expensive. Firms may hire consultants to evaluate the product, particularly when it's the result of innovation or is technologically complex. The market size and competitive position of the company are analyzed by contacts with present and potential customers, suppliers, and others. Production costs are reviewed. The financial condition of the company is confirmed by an auditor. The legal form and registration of the business are checked. Most importantly, the character and competence of the management are evaluated by the venture capital firm, normally via a thorough background check.

These preliminary investigations may cost a venture firm between $2,000 and $3,000 per company investigated. They result in perhaps 10 to 15 proposals of interest. Then, second investigations, more thorough and more expensive than the first, reduce the number of proposals under consideration to only three or four. Eventually the firm invests in one or two of these.

Maturity of the Firm Making the Proposal. Most venture capital firms' investment interest is limited to projects proposed by companies with some operating history, even though they may not yet have shown a profit. Companies that can expand into a new product line or a new market with additional funds are particularly interesting. The venture capital firm can provide funds to enable such companies to grow in a spurt rather than gradually as they would on retained earnings.

Companies that are just starting or that have serious financial difficulties may interest some venture capitalists, if the potential for significant gain over the long run can be identified and assessed. If the venture firm has already extended its portfolio to a large risk concentration, they may be reluctant to invest in these areas because of increased risk of loss.

However, although most venture capital firms will not consider a great many proposals from start-up companies, there are a small number of venture firms that will do only "start-up" financing. The small firm that has a well thought-out plan and can demonstrate that its management group has an outstanding record (even if it is with other companies) has a decided edge in acquiring this kind of seed capital.

Management of the Proposing Firm. Most venture capital firms concentrate primarily on the competence and character of the proposing firm's management. They feel that even mediocre products can be successfully manufactured, promoted, and distributed by an experienced, energetic management group.

They look for a group that is able to work together easily and productively, especially under conditions of stress from temporary reversals and competitive problems. They know that even excellent products can be ruined by poor management. Many venture capital firms really invest in management capability, not in product or market potential.

Obviously, analysis of managerial skill is difficult. A partner or senior executive of a venture capital firm normally spends at least a week at the offices of a company being considered, talking with and observing the management, to estimate their competence and character.

Venture capital firms usually require that the company under consideration have a complete management group. Each of the important functional areas — product design, marketing, production, finance, and control

— must be under the direction of a trained, experienced member of the group. Responsibilities must be clearly assigned. And, in addition to a thorough understanding of the industry, each member of the management team must be firmly committed to the company and its future.

The "Something Special" in the Plan. Next in importance to the excellence of the proposing firm's management group, most venture capital firms seek a distinctive element in the strategy or product/market/process combination of the firm. This distinctive element may be a new feature of the product or process or a particular skill or technical competence of the management. But it **must** exist. It **must** provide a competitive advantage.

Elements of a Venture Proposal

Purpose and Objectives — a summary of the what and why of the project.
Proposed Financing — the amount of money you'll need from the beginning to the maturity of the project proposed, how the proceeds will be used, how you plan to structure the financing, and why the amount designated is required.
Marketing — a description of the market segment you've got or plan to get, the competition, the characteristics of the market, and your plans (with costs) for getting or holding the market segment you're aiming at.
History of the Firm — a summary of significant financial and organizational milestones, description of

employees and employee relations, explanations of banking relationships, recounting of major services or products your firm has offered during its existence, and the like.

Description of the Product or Service — a full description of the product (process) or service offered by the firm and the costs associated with it in detail.

Financial Statements — both for the past few years and pro forma projections (balance sheets, income statements, and cash flows) for the next 3-5 years, showing the effect anticipated if the project is undertaken and if the financing is secured (This should include an analysis of key variables affecting financial performance, showing what could happen if the projected level of revenue is not attained.).

Capitalization — a list of shareholders, how much is invested to date, and in what form (equity/debt).

Biographical Sketches — the work histories and qualifications of key owners/employees.

Principal Suppliers and Customers

Problems Anticipated and Other Pertinent Information — a candid discussion of any contingent liabilities, pending litigation, tax or patent difficulties, and any other contingencies that might affect the project you're proposing.

Advantages — a discussion of what's special about your product, service, marketing plans or channels that gives your project unique leverage.

Provisions of the Investment Proposal

What happens when, after the exhaustive investigation and analysis, the venture capital firm decides to invest in a company? Most venture firms prepare an equity financing proposal that details the amount of money to be provided, the percentage of common stock to be surrendered in exchange for these funds, the interim financing method to be used, and the protective covenants to be included.

This proposal will be discussed with the management of the company to be financed. The final financing agreement will be negotiated and generally represents a compromise between the management of the company and the partners or senior executives of the venture capital firm. The important elements of this compromise are: ownership, control, annual charges, and final objectives.

Ownership. Venture capital financing is not inexpensive for the owners of a small business. The partners of the venture firm buy a portion of the business's equity in exchange for their investment.

This percentage of equity varies, of course, and depends upon the amount of money provided, the success and worth of the business, and the anticipated investment return. It can range from perhaps 10% in the case of an established, profitable company to as much as 80% or 90% for beginning or financially troubled firms.

Most venture firms, at least initially, don't want a position of more than 30% to 40% because they want the owner to have the incentive to keep building the business. If additional financing is required to support business growth, the outsiders' stake may exceed 50%, but investors realize that small business owner-managers can lose their entrepreneurial zeal under those circumstances. In the final analysis, however, the venture firm, regardless of its percentage of ownership, really wants to leave control in the hands of the com-

pany's managers, because it is really investing in that
management team in the first place.

Most venture firms determine the ratio of funds provided to equity requested by a comparison of the present
financial worth of the contributions made by each of the
parties to the agreement. The present value of the contribution by the owner of a starting or financially troubled company is obviously rated low. Often it is estimated
as just the existing value of his or her idea and the competitive costs of the owner's time. The contribution by
the owners of a thriving business is valued much higher.
Generally, it is capitalized at a multiple of the current
earnings and/or net worth.

Financial valuation is not an exact science. The final
compromise on the owner's contribution's worth in the
equity financing agreement is likely to be much lower
than the owner thinks it should be and considerably
higher than the partners of the capital firm think it
might be. In the ideal situation, of course, the two parties to the agreement are able to do together what
neither could do separately: 1) the company is able to
grow fast enough with the additional funds to do more
than overcome the owner's loss of equity, and 2) the investment grows at a sufficient rate to compensate the
venture capitalists for assuming the risk.

An equity financing agreement with an outcome in five
to seven years which pleases both parties is ideal. Since,
of course, the parties can't see this outcome in the present, neither will be perfectly satisfied with the compromise reached.

It is important, though, for the business owner to look at
the future. He or she should carefully consider the im-

pact of the ratio of funds invested to the ownership given up, not only for the present, but for the years to come.

Control. Control is a much simpler issue to resolve. Unlike the division of equity over which the parties are bound to disagree, control is an issue in which they have a common (though perhaps unapparent) interest. While it's understandable that the management of a small company will have some anxiety in this area, the partners of a venture firm have little interest in assuming control of the business. They have neither the technical expertise nor the managerial personnel to run a number of small companies in diverse industries. They much prefer to leave operating control to the existing management.

The venture capital firm does, however, want to participate in any strategic decisions that might change the basic product/market character of the company and in any major investment decisions that might divert or deplete the financial resouces of the company. They will, therefore, generally ask that at least one partner be made a director of the company.

Venture capital firms also want to be able to assume control and attempt to rescue their investments, if severe financial, operating, or marketing problems develop. Thus, they will usually include protective covenants in their equity financing agreements to permit them to take control and appoint new officers if financial performance is very poor.

Annual Charges. The investment of the venture capital firm may be in the final form of direct stock ownership which does not impose fixed charges. More likely, it will be in an interim form—convertible subordinated debentures or preferred stock. Financings may also be straight loans with options or warrants that can be converted to a future equity position at a pre-established price.

The convertible debenture form of financing is like a loan. The debentures can be converted at an established ratio to the common stock of the company within a given period, so that the venture capital firm can prepare to realize their capital gains at their option in the future. These instruments are often subordinated to existing and planned debt to permit the company invested in to obtain additional bank financing.

Debentures also provide additional security and control for the venture firm and impose a fixed charge for interest (and sometimes for principal payment, too) upon the company. The owner-manager of a small company seeking equity financing should consider the burden of any fixed annual charges resulting from the financing agreement.

Final Objectives. Venture capital firms generally intend to realize capital gains on their investments by providing for a stock buy-back by the small firm, by arranging a public offering of stock of the company invested in, or by providing for a merger with a larger firm that has publicly traded stock. They usually hope to do this within five to seven years of their initial investment. (It should be noted that several additional stages of financing may be required over this period of time.)

Most equity financing agreements include provisions guaranteeing that the venture capital firm may participate in any stock sale or approve any merger, regardless of their percentage of stock ownership. Sometimes the agreement will require that the management work toward an eventual stock sale or merger. Clearly, the owner-manager of a small company seeking equity financing must consider the future impact upon his or her own stock holdings and personal ambition of the venture firm's aims, since taking in a venture capitalist as a partner may be virtually a commitment to sell out or go public.

Types of Venture Capital Firms

There is quite a variety of types of venture capital firms. They include:

Traditional partnerships—which are often established by wealthy families to aggressively manage a portion of their funds by investing in small companies;

Professionally managed pools—which are made up of institutional money and which operate like the traditional partnerships;

Investment banking firms—which usually trade in more established securities, but occasionally form investor syndicates for venture proposals;

Insurance companies—which often have required a portion of equity as a condition of their loans to smaller companies as protection against inflation;

Manufacturing companies—which have sometimes looked upon investing in smaller companies as a means of supplementing their R & D programs (Some "Fortune 500" corporations have venture capital operations to help keep them abreast of technological innovations); and

Small Business Investment Corporations (SBIC's)—which are licensed by the Small Business Adminsitration (SBA) and which may provide management assistance as well as venture capital. (When dealing with SBIC's, the small business owner-manager should intially determine if the SBIC is primarily interested in an equity position, as venture capital, or merely in long-term lending on a fully secured basis.)

In addition to these venture capital firms there are individual private investors and finders. Finders, which can be firms or individuals, often know the capital industry and may be able to help the small company seeking capital to locate it, though they are generally not sources of capital themselves. Care should be exercised ,so that a small business owner deals with reputable, professional finders whose fees are in line with industry practice. Further, it should be noted that venture capitalists generally prefer working directly with principals in making investments, though finders may provide useful introductions.

The Importance of Formal Financial Planning

In case there is any doubt about the implications of the previous sections, it should be noted: **It is extremely difficult for any small firm—especially the starting or struggling company—to get venture capital.**

There is one thing, however, that owner-managers of small businesses can do to improve the chances of their venture proposals at least escaping the 90% which are almost immediately rejected. In a word—**plan.**

Having financial plans demonstrates to venture capital firms that you are a competent manager, that you may have that special managerial edge over other small business owners looking for equity money. You may gain a decided advantage through well-prepared plans and projections that include: cash budgets, pro forma statements, and capital investment analysis and capital source studies.

Cash budgets should be projected for one year and prepared monthly. They should combine expected sales revenues, cash receipts, material, labor and overhead expenses, and cash disbursements on a monthly basis. This permits anticipation of fluctuations in the level of cash and planning for **short term** borrowing and investment.

Pro forma statements should be prepared for planning up to 3 years ahead. They should include both income statements and balance sheets. Again, these should be prepared quarterly to combine expected sales revenues; production, marketing, and administrative expenses; profits; product, market, or process investments; and supplier, bank, or investment company borrowings. Pro forma statements permit you to anticipate the financial results of your operations and to plan **intermediate term** borrowings and investments.

Capital investment analyses and capital source studies should be prepared for planning up to 5 years ahead.

The investment analyses should compare rates of return for product, market, or process investment, while the source alternatives should compare the cost and availability of debt and equity and the expected level of retained earnings, which together will support the selected investments. These analyses and source studies should be prepared quarterly so you may anticipate the financial consequences of changes in your company's strategy. They will allow you to plan **long term** borrowings, equity placements, and major investments.

There's a bonus in making such projections. They force you to consider the results of your actions. Your estimates must be explicit; you have to examine and evaluate your managerial records; disagreements have to be resolved—at least discussed and understood. Financial planning may be burdensome but it's one of the keys to business success.

Now, making these financial plans will not guarantee that you'll be able to get venture capital. Not making them, will virtually assure that you won't receive favorable consideration from venture capitalists.

12

Summary Of How To Start A Home-Based Business

Up until recently, going to work meant traveling from home to a plant or office. Today many people do some or all of their work at home. A private market-research firm estimates that as many as 13 million people squeeze extra hours into their work week by taking work home from their full-time jobs, while some 9 million people work exclusively at home.

Many people find that working at home is an ideal arrangement and decide to formally set up businesses there. The SBA estimates that more than 3 million of these home-based businesses are now operating throughout the country.

Every day, people are striking out and achieving economic and creative independence by turning their skills into dollars. Garages, basements and attics are being transformed into the corporate headquarters of the newest entrepreneurs - home-based business people. And with recent technological advances and a rising demand for "service-oriented" businesses, the opportunities seem to be endless.

Is a Home-Based Business Right for You?

Before you dive head first into a home-based business, it's essential that you know why you are doing it and how you will do it. To succeed, your business must be based on something greater than a desire to be your own boss: an honest assessment of your own personality, an understanding of what's involved, and a lot of hard work. You have to be willing to plan ahead, then make improvements and adjustments along the road. While there are no "best" or "right" reasons for starting a home-based business, it is vital to have a very clear idea of what you are getting into and why.

Ask yourself these questions:

- Are you a self-starter?

- Can you stick to business if you're working at home?

- Do you have the necessary self-discipline to maintain schedules?

- Can you deal with the isolation of working from home?

Working under the same roof that your family lives under may not prove to be as easy as it seems. It is important that you work in a professional environment; if at all possible, you should set up a separate office in your home. You must consider if —

- your home has the space for a business, and

- you can successfully run the business from your home.

Legal Requirements

A home-based business is subject to many of the same laws and regulations affecting other businesses - and you will be responsible for complying with them. There are some general areas to watch out for, but be sure to consult an attorney and your state department of labor to find out which laws and regulations will affect your business.

Zoning: Be aware of your city's zoning regulations. If your business operates in violation of them, you could be fined or closed down.

Restrictions on certain goods: Certain products may not be produced in the home. Most states outlaw home production of fireworks, drugs, poisons, explosives, sanitary or medical products, and toys. Some states also prohibit home-based businesses from making food, drink or clothing.

Registration and accounting requirements: You may need a -

- work certificate or a license from the state (your business's name also may need to be registered with the state),

- sales tax number,

- separate business telephone, and

- separate business bank account.

If your business has employees, you are responsible for -

- withholding income and social security taxes, and

- complying with minimum wage and employee health and safety laws.

Finding Your Niche

Choosing a home business is like choosing a spouse or partner — your decision must be approached with a great deal of care. You need to learn as much about the market for any product or service as you can. Before you invest your time, effort and money, take a few moments to answer the following questions. They'll help separate sound ideas from those with a high potential for failure.

- Can you identify and describe the business you plan on establishing?

- What will be your product or service?

- Is there a demand for your product or service?

- What advantages do you have over your competitors?

- Do you have the talent and expertise needed to compete successfully?

Developing A Business Plan

If you've researched your market, thought over the pros and cons of a home-based business, and decided to go ahead, it's time to put together a business plan.

Developing a business plan forces you to take an objective and critical look at your business idea. Even more, the finished product is a tool that will help move your business toward success.

A business plan should be neat, written clearly, and should include several things. The cover page should list the business name, address, mailing address, telephone number and the names of the owner(s). Identify your primary goals and objectives.

Next, give an accurate and concise description of the business:

- What is the principal activity? Be specific. Give product or service descriptions.

- How will the business be started?

- Why will it succeed? Promote your idea. Use your market research.

- What skills and experience do you bring to the business?

Marketing is the core of your business. Carefully think about the following questions, then include your marketing strategy in the business plan:

- Can you market your business from home?

- Who and what is your market?

- What pricing/sales terms are you planning?

- How will you be competitive?

The Financial Plan

Money fuels all businesses. With a little planning, you'll find that you can avoid most financial difficulties.

When drawing up a financial plan, don't worry about using estimates. The process of thinking through these questions helps develop your business skills and leads to solid financial planning.

Start-up costs: To estimate your start-up costs, include all initial expenses such as fees, licenses, permits, telephone deposit, tools, office equipment and promotional expenses. Business experts say you should not expect a profit for the first eight to 10 months, so be sure to give yourself enough cushion.

Projecting operating expenses: Include salaries, utilities, office supplies, loan payments, taxes, legal services and insurance premiums. Don't forget to include your normal living expenses.

Projecting income: It is essential that you know how to estimate your sales on a daily and monthly basis. From the sales estimates, you can develop projected income statements, break-even points and cash-flow statements. Use your marketing research to estimate initial sales volume.

Cash flow: Working capital - not profits - pays your bills. Even though your assets may look great on the balance sheet, if your cash is tied up in receivables or equipment, your business is technically insolvent - in other words, you're broke.

Make a list of all anticipated expenses and projected income for each week and month. If you see a cash-flow crisis developing, cut back on everything but the necessities.

Learn From Others

Remember, preparation is the foundation of success. Talk to home-based business people. Join a home-based-business professional association or "moonlight" at a similar business.

Learn how to use business resources to strengthen your home-based business. Success doesn't just happen - you have to make it happen.

13

Summary Of How To Start A Small Business Outside Your Home

Starting and managing a business takes motivation, desire and talent. It also takes research and planning.

Like a chess game, success in small business starts with decisive and correct opening moves. And although initial mistakes are not fatal, it takes skill, discipline and hard work to regain the advantage.

To increase your chance for success, take the time up front to explore and evaluate your business and personal goals. Then use this information to build a comprehensive and well-thought-out business plan that will help you reach these goals.

The process of developing a business plan will help you think through some important issues that you may not have considered yet. Your plan will become a valuable tool as you set out to raise money for your business. It should also provide milestones to gauge your success.

Getting Started

Before starting out, list your reasons for wanting to go into business. Some of the most common reasons for starting a business are:

- You want to be your own boss.

- You want financial independence.

- You want creative freedom.

- You want to fully use your skills and knowledge.

Next you need to determine what business is "right for you."
Ask yourself these questions:

- What do I like to do with my time?

- What technical skills have I learned or developed?

- What do others say I am good at?

- Will I have the support of my family?

- How much time do I have to run a successful business?

- Do I have any hobbies or interests that are marketable?

Then you should identify the niche your business will fill.
Conduct the necessary research to answer these questions:

- What business am I interested in starting?

- What services or products will I sell?

- Is my idea practical, and will it fill a need?

- What is my competition?

- What is my business's advantage over existing firms?

- Can I deliver a better quality service?

- Can I create a demand for my business?

The final step before developing your plan is the pre-business checklist. You should answer these questions:

- What skills and experience do I bring to the business?

- What will be my legal structure?

- How will my company's business records be maintained?

- What insurance coverage will be needed?

- What equipment or supplies will I need?

- How will I compensate myself?

- What are my resources?

- What financing will I need?

- Where will my business be located?

- What will I name my business?

Your answers will help you create a focused, well-researched business plan. That should serve as a blueprint. It should detail how the business will be operated, managed and capitalized.

The following outline of a typical business plan can serve as a guide, but you should adapt it to your specific business. We recommend that you break down the plan into several components. This allows you to work on several sections at a time.

Business Plan Outline

Introduction

- Give a detailed description of the business and its goals.

- Discuss the ownership of the business and the legal structure.

- List the skills and experience you bring to the business.

- Discuss the advantages you and your business have over your competitors.

Marketing

- Discuss the products/services offered.

- Identify the customer demand for your product/service.

- Identify your market, its size and locations.

- Explain how your product/service will be advertised and marketed.

- Explain the pricing strategy.

Financial Management

- Explain the source and amount of initial equity capital.

- Develop a monthly operating budget for the first year.

- Develop an expected return on investment, or ROI, and monthly cash flow for the first year.

- Provide projected income statements and balance sheets for a two-year period.

- Discuss your break-even point.

- Explain your personal balance sheet and method of compensation.

- Discuss who will maintain your accounting records ? they will be kept.

- Provide "what if" statements that address altern approaches to any problem that may develop

Operations

- Explain how the business will be managed on a day-to-day basis.

- Discuss hiring and personnel procedures.

- Discuss insurance, lease or rent agreements, and issues pertinent to your business.

- Account for the equipment necessary to produce your products or services.

- Account for production and delivery of products and services.

Concluding Statement

- Summarize your business goals and objectives and express your commitment to the success of your business.

Once you have completed your business plan, review it with a friend or business associate. When you feel comfortable with the content and structure, make an appointment to review and discuss it with your banker. The business plan is a flexible document that should change as your business grows.